THE BEGINNINGS OF SOUTH INDIAN HISTORY

THE BEGINNINGS OF SOUTH INDIAN HISTORY

S. KRISHNASWAMI AIYANGAR

GYAN

Published by

GYAN

Gyan Publishing House
5, Ansari Road
Daryaganj, New Delhi-110002
Phone: 011-47034999, 9811692060
E-mail: books@gyanbooks.com

Distribution Network
gyanbooks.com
India, USA, Canada, UK, Australia

ISBN: 978-93-6280-810-3 (PB)
First Published, 1918

2nd Impression 2024

Printed at: Gyan Press, Delhi.

THE BEGINNINGS OF SOUTH INDIAN HISTORY
Author: S. KRISHNASWAMI AIYANGAR

THE BEGINNINGS OF SOUTH INDIAN HISTORY

THE BEGINNINGS OF SOUTH INDIAN HISTORY

S. KRISHNASWAMI AIYANGAR,
PROFESSOR OF INDIAN HISTORY AND ARCHÆOLOGY,
UNIVERSITY OF MADRAS.

MADRAS:
THE MODERN PRINTING WORKS,
MOUNT ROAD.

1918

PREFACE.

The following pages contain the substance of the course of Special Lectures delivered before the University of Madras in January and February of this year. I have also included in this course by way of introduction two other lectures; the first of these was intended to be the inaugural lecture for the University and the second delivered on a previous occasion, both of them bearing directly on the subject of this course. In one or two cases the lecture as delivered was revised to give it the necessary expansion to make it fuller. Otherwise the volume contains no more than the special course of lectures.

The sources of matter for these lectures have often been exploited by fits and starts, for various purposes on occasions by different writers. No one, however, made a constructive critical attempt to make these yield the results they were capable of, except the late Mr. Kanakasabhai Pillai of the Madras Postal Service. His work, giving as it does obvious evidence of great learning and considerable insight, still fell short in the essential particular that each one of the sources tapped was not subjected to a detailed criticism in respect of its historical worth. Notwithstanding this defect it is monumental work which deserves better of the Tamilian though his conclusions may not all of them stand the test of time and criticism. Since his time we have advanced considerably, and most of the classics have been edited critically by Pandits who deserve public thanks for the labour and learning brought to bear upon the work. Improvements are certainly possible and will surely come if some interest is evinced in the results of that work. The names of Pandit Mahamahopadhyaya Swaminatha Aiyar of Madras, the late Pandit Binnattūr Narayanaswami Aiyar of Kumbhakoṇam and Pandit Rangaswami Aiyangar of Vaniambadi deserve special mention in this connection. It gives me the greatest pleasure to acknowledge my obligation to their work. I should not forget, however, another labourer of an elder generation, the late Mr. C. W. Thamotharam Pillai to whose loving labours we are indebted for a number of Tamil works which otherwise would have been ordinarily inaccessible.

In regard to the late Mr. Kanakasabhai's work a criticism was fashionable that his work was 'patriotic'. It was Johnson that said 'Patriotism is the last resort of the scoundrel.' This remark of the great Doctor may have had its application in his time and may not be altogether without it in other times. The late Mr. Kanakasabhai might have let his patriotism get the better of his judgment on occasions. I have carefully tried to avoid laying myself open to such a heavy charge. My trouble has been the difficulty of making facts already known agree with those we may arrive at. This is a test not always applied in recent investigations and both the statement of facts so-called, and the suppressing of those that may be inconvenient, have in some cases gone together. I have tried scrupulously to avoid both, though both errors of omission and commission are possible. Too much has been attempted to be made of epigraphical evidence recently, and the late Mr. Venkayya's name was quoted against me in the connection. I had known the late Mr. Venkayya for near a score of years before his lamented death, and I may even say that I am obliged to him for a part of the inspiration that ultimately led me to this field of work. Mr. Venkayya was in substantial agreement with me in regard to the general position, but he had his doubts as to the Śilappadikāram and Maṇimēkhalai being of the same age. I am almost certain that had he lived now, he would have accepted, the conclusions I have arrived at. I leave the reader to judge for himself in regard to these conclusions ; all I wish to state here is that I have not allowed 'patriotism' to take command of evidence.

In regard to the evidence of this body of material a few words may usefully be said here. The whole collection of literature that goes by the collective name 'Śangam Works,' is of the nature of anthologies with few exceptions. They were occasional poems, the objects of which were generally the celebration of the achievements of patrons. Having regard to this character of theirs they are sometimes very outspoken ; but generally they shew a tendency to 'add another hue unto the rainbow.' It is, however, easily possible to allow for the panegyrist in the poet. These poems fall into two classes according to the conventions of Tamil Rhetoric. Those relating to the 'field of action' are direct and connect themselves with specific events and incidents in the life of the patron. Those 'dealing with emotion' are less direct in regard to the points of reference, but they have to celebrate something connected with the achievements of the actual patron addressed or that of his ancestors. Judiciously used the latter provide material as valuable as the former does. The only comparison possible in respect of these is the pre-

Homeric lays or the bardic tales of the days of chivalry in Europe, or even India. There are about twenty collections that will go into this class. Of these all but two of the more important have been printed. The others remain yet to be published.

In the use of this wealth of material, which undoubtedly is of the nature of contemporary evidence, what is required is such a general study as would give an idea of the 'general lie of the land' before specific use of the material is attempted. Much of the work that is generally done suffers from a want of this preliminary equipment. In the following pages I have had it before me all the time to avoid this. How far I have achieved success, it is not for me to say.

I take advantage of this preface to make clear two points in the work which seem ambiguous. On p. 48 Pinna Timma is referred to as the grandson of Ramaraja. This latter is likely to be understood as the Ramaraja who fell at Talikota. The next following sentences seem to confirm this impression. Both Pinna Timma and Rama of Talikota were alike grandsons of another Rama Raja, who served with distinction under Narasa and his son Vīra—Narasimha. Pinna Timma and his brother Viṭṭala were fisst cousins of Ramarāja, and conducted the expedition to the South and organised the Madura Province under Sadasiva and Ramaraja. The next point calling for remark here is on p. 223 where the first sentence, beginning on this page, refers to the absence of mention of Pattini in the poem under discussion. It is quite likely that this was due to the fact that this poem was written before Śenguṭṭuvan's northern invasion and the building of the temple of Pattini which came after the 50th year of his reign, when the others of his achievements discussed had become well known—(vide Śilappadikāram canto XXVII. ll. 118-128 & ll. 165-175).

I have the greatest pleasure here in acknowledging my obligations to the Syndicate of the Madras University for having sanctioned the expenses of copying for my use the Ahanānūru manuscript in the Government Manuscripts Library; to Rai Sahib H. Krishna Sastrigal for his kindness in lending me the impressions and the office transcripts of two valuable Pāṇḍya grants: namely the Vēlvikkudi grant, and the larger Sinnamanur Plates; and to Pandit Maha. Swaminatha Aiyar for having been at the trouble to copy and supply me with two of the valuable poems in the collection from his excellently collated text of the Ahanānūru. I am equally obliged to Mr. M. K. Srinivasa Aiyangar, the Proprietor of the Modern Printing Works, for having cheerfully undertaken the publication of this work, and for having done it so well, putting the work through the Press in less than three weeks. One of my research students, Mr. N. R. Saṭṭanathan, B. A. (Hons.) took the trouble of preparing the index and the errata which it was found impossible to avoid owing to the rapidity with which the work went through the Press. I acknowledge with pleasure my indebtedness to him for these good offices.

MADRAS,
1st March 1918. S. KRISHNASWAMI AIYANGAR.

CONTENTS.

INTRODUCTORY

I

RESEARCH IN INDIAN HISTORY

WHAT HISTORY IS

'HISTORY is fable agreed upon' was how history was understood at one time when the idea of history primarily as a piece of literature held sway. We have since gone a long way from that position. Without attempting to set forth what history is, a task which baffled the genius of far greater men than I am, I may make an extract from one of the leading thinkers of the day on matters germane thereto, to gain an idea of what is actually understood by the term. Lord Morley has it in his Notes on Politics and History, 'History, in the great conception of it, has often been compared to a mountain chain seen far off in a clear sky, where the peaks seem linked towards one another towards the higher crest of the group. An ingenious and learned writer the other day amplified this famous image, by speaking of a set of volcanic islands heaving themselves out of the sea, at such angles and distances that only to the eye of a bird, and not to a sailor cruising among them, would they appear as the heights of one and the same submerged range. The sailor is the politician. The historian, without prejudice to monographic exploration in intervening valleys and ascending slopes, will covet the vision of the bird.

SHORTCOMINGS OF HISTORICAL STUDY

Discussing the distinction between ancient and modern history on this basis, Lord Morley passes on to some of the shortcomings of historical study at the present time, and makes the following observations commenting on specialization: "We may find comfort in the truth that though excess of specialization is bad, to make sciolism into a system is worse. In reading history it is one common fault to take too short measure of the event, to mistake some early scene in the play as if it were the fifth act, and so conceive the plot all amiss. The event is only comprehended in its fullest dimensions, and for that the historic recorder, like or unlike the actor before him, *needs insight and imagination*." Further on, the same great authority says: 'All agree that we have no business to seek more from the past than the very past itself. Nobody disputes with Cicero when he asks: "Who does not know that it is the first law of history not to dare a word that is false? Next, not to shrink from a word that is true. No partiality, no grudge." Though nobody disputes the obvious answers, have a majority of historical practitioners complied?'

HISTORY OF HINDU INDIA

These extracts are quite enough to indicate on the one hand what history is according to the most enlightened modern opinion and on the other, what difficulties confront a labourer—a journeyman labourer—in the vast fields of that history in India as yet but little explored. Even from the coveted height of the eagle if one casts his eyes upon the history of Hindu India one feels—one hardly sees enough even of the volcanic islands, and the few that he might be able to see, one feels he sees but too dimly through the mist of age and increasing distance. It is notorious that India has but little history of her own.

WANT OF CHRONOLOGY

It was the illustrious historian of India, Elphinstone, that observed in 1839 that, in regard to Indian History, 'no date of a public event can be fixed before the invasion of Alexander; and no connected relation of the national transaction can be attempted until after the Muhammadan conquest.' Cowell extended the application of this caution to the whole of the Hindu Period, writing as he did in 1866. During the next half century we have advanced from this position a long way indeed, and VINCENT A. SMITH'S *Early History of India* is the most substantial vindication of the possibility of compiling a connected history of Hindu India, but even so much advance does not invalidate the first part of Elphinstone's dictum.

AN OXFORD CHAIR FOR INDIAN HISTORY ONLY BRITISH CONNECTION

It is nearly half a century since, that the first attempt was made at Oxford to institute a chair or something near it, for the study of Indian History; but the work of this foundation was, however, limited to the history of the British connection with India. The inaugural address delivered in January 1914 by the present occupant of this position, Rev. William Holden Hutton, B. D., contains the following appeal anent this question: He (the Reader) is instructed by statute to lecture on "The Rise, Growth and Organization of the British Power in India." This leads me to say what I think very much needs saying to-day. It is a grievous weakness in the University's provision for learning that there is nothing done for the study of Indian History in ancient and mediæval times. I should like to direct the attention of those who have the control of the Chancellor's Fund to this strange omission. A period of the world's history of extraordinary interest and of really enormous importance is entirely neglected in our provision for learning, education and research. It is true that we have distinguished scholars who have, from time to time, dealt with a part of this subject, such as Professor Macdonnell and Mr. Vincent A. Smith; but the former has already a subject so wide that only his knowledge and energy could adequately deal with it, while the latter has, I deeply regret to say, no official position in our midst.

NO PROVISION FOR GENERAL INDIAN STUDIES

Purely Indian History, with its literature and philosophy, Indian Geography, historical and descriptive, (except so far as I am told to deal with it) a subject of extraordinary fascination in itself, Indian archæology, are unprovided for in this University. In spite of the generosity which created, and has, from time to time, enriched the Indian Institute, it still fails to play the important part it might play, and was intended to play, in the education at Oxford. What the Chancellor of the University said in 1909 is, I am afraid, still true.

THE INDIAN INSTITUTE

'The Institute has not in any appreciable degree provided a meeting-ground for the East and West, or a place of social intercourse between English and Indian students. Its Museum has failed 'to bring together a typical collection of objects suited to educational purposes and sufficiently complete to give a fair idea of the industrial occupations, domestic and religious customs of the people subject to our rule;' or 'to present a fair epitome of India, eminently attractive not only to indologists, but to ethnologists and anthropologists of all nationalities.' The scheme of constant lectures by distinguished Anglo-Indian administrators and Orientalists which started under happy auspices, has fallen into desuetude. The Institute possesses no permanent endowment, and is ill-provided in respect of staff and attendance, besides being quite unable to extend its sphere of influence.'

THE DEMAND OF THE GREATEST OF OXFORD HISTORIANS (BISHOP STUBBS)

I believe that this is largely due to the fact that we have still left unheeded the declaration of the greatest of Oxford historians, made so long ago as 1876, when Mr. Sidney Owen had been teaching Indian History in Oxford for eight years. 'At the present moment we want', then said the Regius Professor of Modern History (after proclaiming another need which is still, as I think most disastrously, unsatisfied) :—

"We want a permanent chair of Indian History. The labours of our friend, the present Indian Reader, have shown us how thoroughly that study, the importance of which can scarcely be over-rated by Englishmen, falls in with the current of our University work. I say a permanent chair, because that is a subject of permanent necessity, not a subject like palæography or numismatology, in which the labours of one good professor may serve for two or three generations, and the endowment of the man is of equal importance with the endowment of the chair or study."

That demand of Dr. Stubbs, made nearly forty years ago, is not yet met. I appeal to those whose interest in India is real, who desire that her history should be fully known and rightly understood, who desire that she should be recognised in her greatness among the nations, to Indian princes, and to Europeans who have made fortunes in India, to provide for the creation of a Professorship of Indian History in the University which is already so clearly linked, and could be linked more closely, to the Indian Empire.

THE SAME NEED FOR INDIA

This was the demand made for Oxford forty years ago, already provided with some kind of equipment to meet this particular need. Thanks to the Universities Act of 1904 and the enlightened generosity of the Government of India it has become possible for us now to think of doing something to reclaim that part of the history of our country of which the distant Oxford Professors of History shewed themselves so solicitous nearly half a century ago.

THE MATERIAL AVAILABLE FOR MEETING THIS NEED

The difficulties that have to be overcome in any work of research in this field are many and require talents of the highest order over a wide field of study. Broadly speaking the sources of Indian History can be grouped into three broad classes, namely :—

I. Indian Literature (Traditionary and Historical) ;

II. Foreign Literature, chiefly the works of travellers, &c.;

III. Archæology, Monumental, Numismatic and Epigraphic.

I. INDIAN LITERATURE

The first of these classes falls naturally into two groups, namely, (*a*) Ordinary literature, embodying traditional history in regard to striking incidents and personalities. These find casual mention in works with no historical object of any kind and will be of invaluable service in the construction of history. The chief difficulty that besets the subject here is the absence of any chronological clue which many of the classical works of literature want generally, either in Sanskrit or in our Dravidian Vernaculars. There are some works which, either in the preface or in a colophon at the end of the work, give invariably the name and ancestors of the author, sometimes also the name and ancestry similarly of the patron; and occasionally the date of composition or completion of the work. Where this clue is available the work is of some value to the historian—not generally for history as it is ordinarily understood, Political History—but as throwing some side-light upon a social, religious or other feature of general history

ARRANGEMENT UPON A CHRONOLOGICAL SCHEME

The greater part of the literature of the country has first of all to be carefully studied critically and arranged on a well-planned chronological scheme. This is true alike of Sanskrit and Vernacular literature—the only difference being that in regard to Sanskrit some work has already been done, while in regard to the Dravidian languages which are of material importance to the history of this part of the country, the work has hardly received attention except in very rare instances. To the aspiring historian of South India this will prove the first preliminary spade work essential to any undertaking. He has unfortunately to deal with not any one language but with three, four or five languages, according to the period and the locality to which he directs his ambition and his attention. It is here co-operation and combination, in the shape of a school of workers in history is required, each one of whom limiting his ambition to contributing to the main result without special recognition or reward for each brick he might have directly contributed to make.

PROFESSEDLY HISTORICAL WORKS

The next department of the literature of the country that has here to be taken into consideration is the purely historical literature—a department in which, so far as the available materials go—India is peculiarly weak, so much so that we often hear it said that the faculty for history is utterly absent in India. Bearing in mind that history as we understand the term now is practically the work of nineteenth-century Europe, we can still say with justice that Europe, is well provided with historical literature for many ages and many countries. So it is even with China. In regard to India we can hardly say the same, and when we limit our vision to the south we can almost say there is none such at all. The absence of professed histories does not necessarily imply the absence of historical material in literature. There is much of that kind of ore that can be mined in literature, but it requires the smelting furnace of criticism, with plenty of oxydising material in the shape of chronological data from other sources, and slag of confirmatory evidence to separate the facts from the figments of imagination in which these get embedded. Much of this is true even of the few professed histories that we possess. The typical examples of such are Kalhana's Rājatarangiṇi, Bāṇa's Harsha Charitam and Bilhaṇa's Vikramānkadeva Charitam for Sanskrit, the Kongudeś'a Rājākkal in Tamil and various other smaller historical pieces found in the Mackenzie Manuscripts collection. There is the Rājāvalikathe in Kanarese, and the various historical chronicles of Buddhist history that we have for Ceylon.

Their Value as Historical Material

Various other smaller compositions might be brought under this class, as they deal often with topics contemporaneous with the writers themselves. These, however, and most other of the works already referred to had not the writing of history as their object, and would be more liable to the charge contained in the quotation with which I started that 'History is fable agreed upon.' On the whole these two connected sources do offer to the critical student valuable historical material, neglect of which would make any history of the country, of a higher conception or lower, almost impossible.

The Work that Lies Ahead

Without entering into any detailed description of the various works of a historical character, or attempting to appraise their relative worth as contributing to history, I feel called upon to point out that the work that lies ahead here, almost immediately in front of us, is a critical examination of these, and their presentation in the form of a connected description, so as ultimately to lead up to the writing of a hand-book of literature for each of the literatures of these Dravidian languages on the lines of similar works for European languages we have in such number and variety. When this is done it will be found that the amplitude of the material available for history is much more than we imagine at first-sight.

II. FOREIGN SOURCES OF INDIAN HISTORY

Greek

Passing on to the next division, 'Foreign sources of Indian History' we have here a very large number of contributories in regular succession beginning almost with the Father of History, Herodotus. For Northern India we have a number of Greek accounts of varying degrees of value historically from the age of Herodotus to the days of Asoka almost, and when this begins to fail, Chinese sources begin to appear, about the beginning of the

Christian era. Of the Greek sources I may just mention besides Herodotus, Ktesias, Megasthenes and Arrian, not to mention Quinctus Curtius and Appollonious of Tyana.

Chinese

Of Chinese sources there is the Chinese Father of History Ssu-ma-ch'ien in the first century B. C. and from that time a large number of travellers came almost up to the Muhammadan conquest. Of these we need only mention the well-known ones, Fa-hien at the beginning of the fifth century and Hiuen Thsang in the middle of the seventh. Excepting this last none of the foreign sources cited above have anything but an occasional reference to South India. There is besides the recently discovered Tibetan sources which have not yet been adequately worked up to be of use to the student.

For South India

Under this head South India is not without its own share of illumination from outside. Megasthenes has a few references about the south. There is the Geographer Pliny, then comes in chronological order the unknown author of the Periplus of the Erythraean Sea, and then Ptolemy. Past this period we are able to derive some valuable information from Hiuen Thsang. Last of all there is Marco Polo. For periods later than this we have the Muhammadan travellers, some of them are of very great value, such as Ibn Batutah and Abdur Razak. There are besides a number of other European travellers that came to some part of the southern coast or the interior, Nicolo-dei-Conti who was a contemporary of Deva Raya I, Varthema, the Portuguese traders Nuniz and Paes, and others.

These Shed but Intermittent Light

With very few exceptions the light that these throw upon the history of the country is anything but continuous, and often the information that we gain of the best among them can be regarded as of value only when we have other sources of information to control them. All the same we owe it to them that we have recovered a few bright chapters of South Indian History, and we must acknowledge our obligations to the disinterested labour of European savants to whom entirely is due the credit of having made these available to us.

MUHAMMADAN HISTORIANS

I have so far not made any mention of the Muhammadan historians as a class: For the later period of Hindu History of South India these historians are of considerable importance as outside sources, though hitherto they were the only sources. I class them as outside; for none of them, of design, write the history of any State of Hindu India. Such reference as they make are only incidental and bring them in in the course of the history of the particular Muhammadan State or States whose history they attempt to write. These again have been made available for use by us by an elder generation of European scholars, though there is still room for good scholarly work left upon these.

ARCHÆOLOGICAL SOURCES

(I) MONUMENTAL

We come last of all to the sources, archæological. These have been divided into (1) monumental, (2) numismatic and (3) epigraphic.

These monuments in the shape of buildings, temples and structures of various kinds throw very considerable light upon the religion, art and civilization in general of the particular period to which they belong. They also let us in into the secrets of history in regard to the various influences, foreign or local, that may have had operation in the production of these monuments. To be able to study these monuments, these monuments must exist. So work in this branch of archæology, as a necessary preliminary, takes the character of an organisation for the preservation of those monuments that are visible; then it requires an organisation to carry on work in search for new monuments, and the exposition of those that may be available for study.

Private Effort Impossible in this Line

In a vast country like ours and having regard to the character and condition of these monuments as they are, this becomes particularly a branch of study which does not lend itself at all to private work in regard to its first branch ; the second branch of it, research work in monuments, may to some extent be done by private workers but even in this branch organised work is so necessary for utility that it is only rich societies or Governments that can undertake the conservation and research work satisfactorily, where the latter involve as in the case of the Taxila excavations, or excavations carried on at present at Pāṭalipura, a large outlay of expenditure. After a period of neglect, work upon this branch was undertaken by General Cunningham in the sixties of the last century as Director-General ; but his work was confined to Northern and Central India. A decade later came on an expansion under Burgess when the whole of India was included for work. In either case these officers and their staff confined themselves to research work alone which is embodied in the volumes of Archæological Survey XXII by the first, and XXXIII by the second. A first shy attempt was made at conservation of existing monuments in 1881, and ultimately, thanks to the exertion of various influences, a more comprehensive scheme was put into force at the beginning of the new century, and we are now on a further step forward in the development of archæological work as the Government of India Resolution on the subject indicates.

Numismatics: Largely Private Effort so far

It is in the second branch of archæological work that private effort is quite possible to a very large extent, and a great deal of work has already been done. There are very good collections of coins, seals, &c., in the various museums in India and elsewhere. They have all been carefully studied and catalogued, in addition to much private work that has already been done. It is possible that this may turn out to be a costly fad to an individual but under proper direction it need not be quite so costly at all.

Invaluable to the Chronology of Particular Periods

Costly or otherwise it is a very useful fad and many parts of Indian History have become possible only by the study of coins, and several others have received much needed chronological assistance therefrom.

EPIGRAPHY

Lastly we come to epigraphy, which for the part of the country with which we are directly concerned, is the most important of these sources, and which has reclaimed to us lost history in regard to various periods, localities and dynasties. For the period anterior to A. D. 400 these records obtained so far, are not very many for South India. The total for the whole of India, both North and South, is about 1100 to 1200.

Records Preponderate in Number in South India for Periods After A.D. 400

For the period on this side of A.D. 400 the number already brought to notice up to 1906, when the late Professor Kielhorn compiled his indexes to the inscriptions, is about 700 for

Northern India and 1090 for the South. There have since been added to these the-yearly, collections of which it is only a comparatively small number that has yet been placed before the public in a shape to be dealt with in that manner.

LARGE NUMBERS OF THESE RECORDS

Dr. Fleet, one of the greatest authorities in Indian Epigraphy, has it, 'And, whereas new records are every year being freely obtained in Northern India it is known there is in Southern India a wealth of material the extent of which can hardly yet be gauged.' According to the same authority the collection of transcripts made by Sir Walter Elliott was 595 from the Kanarese country, besides a considerable number from the Telugu Districts. These are placed in the libraries of the Royal Asiatic Society, London, and the University of Edinburgh. Dr. Hultzsch had collected and edited about 300 inscriptions in the first two volumes of South Indian inscriptions, and about an equal number has been added since to the same publication by the issue of one more part of volume II and two of Vol. III, by his successors, the late Mr. Venkayya and Rai Sahib H. Krishna Sastri. Mr. Rice brought out about 9000 inscriptions in the Epigraphia Carnāṭaka and his successor, Mr. R. Narasimhachariar, has added a considerable number to these, though he has not published them in the same form as his predecessor had done. Dr. Fleet has collected about 1000 and placed them all in the Bombay Museum. He further states that 'the southernmost parts of Dharwar which abound with such materials, and some parts of Belgaum and Bijapur Districts, and the Nizam's Dominions still remain to be explored. And a great mass of material from the eastern parts of Southern India.'

Their Value

Apart from this copiousness these inscriptions have a historical value which is all their own. They vary in substance from the simple record of the death of a rural hero who fell fighting in a cattle raid or of his widow's immolation on the pyre of her husband, to a detailed account of a battle or a treaty. If it happens to be a donative offering to a temple or a Brahman it not merely gives genealogical details of the donor and donee, but very often elaborate details of rural administration. Sometimes we come upon records of how justice was administered, in these very documents. In regard to the simpler details of history these records describe them concisely and accurately, and being not deliberately set out as history are all the more reliable. A great number of these records are precisely dated in some one era or another, or in regnal years of the sovereign for the time being. Thus they give us an amount of information of such a character that ordinary histories even of a modern character will not usually give us; so that it is possible to construct from the inscriptions alone something more than mere political history. Thanks to the exertions of various scholars of the passing generation, we have all the various Indian eras in use equated to the Christian era and tables constructed to give equivalent dates.

Co-ordination of Work Desirable

These records, available to us in such large numbers, have made it possible to compile a political history of India from the first century B.C. onwards with sufficient fullness up to the fourth century A. D. and with greater fullness afterwards. But to make the best use of these records and get them to yield all the results they are capable of yielding work in this line will have to go hand in hand with work in other departments of research 'in which hardly a beginning has been made, beyond a preliminary treatment, in detached writings, of details which will have to be hereafter brought together and handled on broader lines in connected and more easily accessible works.'

Fleet's Two Desiderata: (i) Research in Monuments

Dr. Fleet calls for two lines of work of which we have promise, one being taken up systematically and in a more liberal spirit than heretofore, in the Government of India Resolution on Archæology, namely research work in monuments by excavation. This is very necessary to supplement the rather meagre information available for periods anterior to A.D. 320.

(ii) REVISED CORPUS OF INSCRIPTIONS

The next desideratum to which he calls attention is the revision and republication of the Epigraphic material available in a single corpus, *Corpus Inscriptionem Indicarum of* which a beginning was made in the only two volumes so far published, Vol. I, The Inscriptions of Asoka by General Sir Alexander Cunningham, and Volume III, The Gupta Inscriptions, by Dr. Fleet himself. The need certainly is very great.

COLLATION OF OTHER MATERIALS FOR HISTORY

Along with this work has to go on work upon the collation of all historical material available in literature, numismatics, art works, &c., and unless all of these are examined carefully and the material that can be drawn from them made available in a form accessible to students of history, no historical work proper would be possible. This will involve great labour in the literatures of four or five languages, in thousands of inscriptions in all these languages, besides the monuments, coins and works of art generally.

SYMPATHETIC STUDY OF INDIAN ART

It is a hopeful sign of the times that these last are coming in for their share of attention at the hands of some individuals and Governments, and what is more they are coming to be studied with more of that sympathy which hitherto was notoriously wanting. In the words of Justice Woodroffe: "It has been the fashion amongst European art-critics to decry the merits of Brahmanical sculpture on the ground of the alleged monstrosities of the Hindu *pauranic* conceptions, which, it has been said, are incapable of artistic treatment. The examples collected in this volume* will, it is hoped, help to dispel such misconceptions and to refute the unjust criticisms which they have engendered, and will further a juster appreciation of the fact that Indian Sculpture is not a freak of Asiatic barbarism, but is a

* South Indian Bronzes by O. C. Gangooly.

worthy representative of a school of æsthetic performance as logical, articulate and highly developed as those of any country in Europe, ancient or modern."

Vincent A. Smith's "History Fine Art in India and Ceylon," Havell's "Ancient and Medieval Architecture," Gopinatha Rao's "Hindu Iconography," Gangooly's "South Indian Bronzes" and a more systematic work upon a narrower field of work, only the Tamil country, namely "South Indian Architecture and Iconography" by Professor Jouveau-Dubreuil of Pondicherry, all works of recent years do but indicate the rising interest in this line of work.

Universities Shew Interest

It is therefore none too soon that the University of Madras, along with a few others of her sister Universities, resolved to utilise the liberal annual grant of the Government of India for starting a school of Indian studies by instituting Professorships and Readerships in Indian History and Languages having reference to South India chiefly. The success or failure of this scheme depends upon the interest it can evoke and the co-operation it can enlist from among the *alumni* of the University—past and present.

In calling for sympathetic interest and co-operation particularly from the University students here, I cannot do better than quote from Professor Maitland the words in which he once expressed the needs of historical study, 'needs which are nowhere more explicit and evident than in regard to India.'

'More co-operation, more organisation, more and better criticism, more advise for beginners, are needed. And the need, if not met, will increase. History is lengthening and widening, and deepening. It is lengthening at both ends, for while modern States in many parts of the world are making history at a bewilderingly rapid rate, what used to be called ancient history is no longer, by any means, the ancientest; Egypt, Assyria, Babylonia, and even primeval man, are upon our hands. And history is widening. Could we neglect India, China and Japan, there would be still America, Australia, Africa, as well as

Europe, demanding that their stories should be told, and finding men to tell them well or to tell them badly. And history is deepening. We could not, if we would, be satisfied with the battles and the protocols, the alliances and the intrigues. Literature and art, religion and law, rents and prices, creeds and superstitions have burst the political barrier and are no longer to be expelled. The study of interactions and interdependences is but just beginning and no one can foresee the end. *There is much to be done by schools of history*: there will be more to be done every year.'

Co-operation in this particular line is easier for us as the languages that have to be mastered are many and the knowledge that would be really useful is a deep knowledge of one or more of these. The other technical details in the present state of work in the subject are admittedly easy of acquisition. Indian talent comes in very handy in archæological work and ought to be offered largely and accepted liberally. It is only then that the school of Indian studies will become a realised ambition. I leave it in the hands of the younger members of this audience either to realise this ambition or face the alternative of the eternal want of historic sense.

II

THE VALUE OF LITERATURE IN THE CONSTRUCTION OF INDIAN HISTORY

IT is a notorious fact that Indian literature has few professed histories, and the inference seems warranted that the historical faculty received no development in the country. History, as we understand it, is entirely a product of the nineteenth century even in Europe. Works which constitute good material for history have been many, whatever their shortcomings from the point of view of the modern historian. It is in the sense of professed histories which may be subjected to criticism and used as material, that histories are wanting in India.

So the problem of constructing the history of India as a whole, or of any part of it, is subject to this additional defect. Defective it may be and much more so than in European countries. Still there is ample material yet left, despite much vandalism which may yield good results if exploited systematically. Historical material in India as elsewhere, may be grouped into three classes :—

(*I*) *Archæological* (*including architecture*).

(*II*) *Epigraphical* (*including numismatics*).

(*III*) *Literature.*

Of these the first goes back to the earliest times reached in this country by historical research. What can be gathered from this source is, however, scanty though reaching to the earliest antiquity. The second does not go beyond the period of the Asoka Inscriptions. For periods anterior to this, we are thrown upon literature only, both Vedic and Buddhistic. With respect to South India also archæological evidence may take us farther back, but the epigraphical does not go back beyond the beginning of the Christian Era except for a few Asoka and Sātavāhana records. Whether literature will take us beyond this limit may well be regarded doubtful, as we are at present, but careful research in this direction may take us past this limit and may yield us results beyond our expectations. I have not set myself to inquire here whether it is so, nor whether all literary evidence has been brought to bear on historical research. I shall only try to show that the inquiry will not be in vain if it is made.

This inquiry necessarily leads us to the question of languages. For any work of research concerning India, Sanskrit is indispensable. This is clear from what we know of the pre-Buddhistic period of Indian history. When we come to deal with South India, Tamil becomes equally essential. Of the other Dravidian languages, Telugu does not take its available literature much anterior to the ninth century A.D., and this literature seems to be modelled upon Sanskrit entirely. Kanarese has certainly a more ancient literature. A work of the ninth century undoubtedly is the Kavirājamārga of Nṛipatunga. If a work of poetics like this had been written in the ninth century, we might presume that there was an amount of anterior literature to require this. Malayalam seems to have grown out of Tamil in the early centuries of the Christian Era. But Tamil which, according to some, is the mother of these three, goes back to a far greater antiquity. It has a wealth of literature for particular periods which is worth study on scientific lines. This body of literature, independent of Sanskrit and yet so closely interwoven with it, deserves well of those who wish to be among the educated of their country's sons. It may not be all who can afford to study it, but those who can ought not to neglect to do so. How is this vast literature, both Sanskrit and Dravidian, to be exploited to any purpose, and what is likely to be the utility of such exploitation for history?

I began with the statement that history depends upon archæology, epigraphy and literature for its materials. The work on the first two has been considered to belong to the province of Government, for it is beyond the resources of private work, though private agency may do much if facilities are provided. Work upon the third is so far left entirely to the patriotic lovers of literature. It is not literature as literature that is my concern here, but literature so far as it can be of use for the making of history.

That literature can provide for history needs no proof now. The study of the literature of Pāḷi, the vernacular of a part of Northern India in the centuries before Christ, opened to us a fresh vista into the domain of the history of ancient India. Will the Dravidian languages similarly open another vista? It is this question I shall attempt to answer here, confining my observations to Tamil literature, the oldest and the most voluminous of these southern tongues, as they are at present. That a systematic study of this literature will yield results of great value even where one least expects it, I can illustrate from the following incident in the life of Rāmānuja, the Vaishṇava apostle.

Tradition states, and the *Guruparamparais* (histories of apostolic succession) record, that Rāmānuja constructed the temple at the town of Tirupati, and enshrined the image of Govindarāja there. This image was believed to have been the image of Govindarāja at Chidambaram, pulled out of the temple and cast into the sea by a certain Chola king, called

Krimikaṇṭa by the Vaishṇavas, a persecuting Chola. So far as I know at present, there seems to be no inscription bearing upon this question, and the matter was believed to be traditional and nothing more. It was asserted in a court of law that the existence of the Vishṇu shrine at Chidambaram was due to the pious fraud of a Vaishṇava Brahman, who planted the image of Vishṇu over night, and duped the people, who woke up one morning to find the image of Vishṇu in the Śaiva (Holy of Holies). If the witness himself believed in it, as in honesty we are bound to grant he did, he must have been a credulous person indeed. We are not concerned with his credulity or otherwise, but we are with the credibility of the tale. Stanza 86 [1] of the Tiruchchiṟṟambalakkōvai of Māṇikkavāśagar states in the words of the devotee that Vishṇu was lying in the court yard of the temple at Chidambaram supplicating Śiva, when, in response

1 புரங்கடந் தானடி காண்பான் புவிவிண்டு புக்கறியா
இரங்கிடென் றாயென் றிரப்பத்தன் னீரடிக் கென்னிரண்டு
கரங்கடந் தானொன்று காட்ட மற்றாங்கதுங் காட்டிடென்று
வரங்கிடந் தான்றில்லை யம்பல முன்றிலம் மாயவனே.

to Vishṇu's prayer, after fruitlessly penetrating the earth to discover the feet of Śiva, he displayed one foot, that he might show the other as well. This is a clever description of the relative positions and postures of the two deities in the temple. Naṭēsa is in his self-forgetful dance with his right foot lifted up. Govindarāja is in his bhōgaśayana (reclining posture).

Kulasēkhara Āḻvār states regarding the same Govindarāja that Vishṇu was recumbent on a throne, with the three thousand Brahmans chanting his praise in the Chitrakūṭa of Tillai city, surrounded by cool and shady gardens, smiling with flowers and tender shooṭs.

Next comes what Tirumangai Āḻvar says about the same:—

The first extract [3] simply indicates that a

2 செந்தளிர்வாய் மலர்நகைசேர் செழுந்தண் சோலைத்
தில்லைநகர்த் திருச்சித்ர கூடந் தன்னு
ளந்தணர்க ளொருமூவா யிரவ ரேத்த
வணிமணியா சனத்தமர்ந்த வம்மான் றானே.

3 பைம்பொன்னு முத்தும் மணியுங் கொணர்ந்து
படைமன்னவர் பல்லவர் கோன்ப ணிந்த
செம்பொன்மணி மாடங்கள் சூழ்ந்த தில்லைத்
திருச்சித்ர கூடஞ்சென்று சேர்மின்களே.

Pallava king made some costly dedications to the temple. The second [4] that Vishṇu was in a lying posture on his serpent couch. The third [5] that the three thousand of Tillai worshipped, according to orthodox rights, the God of Gods.

Thus, then, in the days of the two Āḷvārs and Māṇikkavāśagar, the Vishṇu shrine occupied the position that it does now. Let us proceed then to a later period, the period of the later Cholas. The Chola decline may be dated as commencing with the death of Kulōttunga Chola I. He was succeeded by his son Vikramachola; and he by his son Kulōttunga II, who was succeeded by Raja Rāja II. The poet called Oṭṭakkūttan, there are reasons for believing, was a contemporary

4 ஒருமா கடலுட் கிடந்தா னுவந்து
கவைநா வரவி னணைப்பள்ளி யின்மேல்
திருமால் திருமங்கை யோடாடு தில்லைத்
திருச்சித்ர கூடம்.

5 மூவா யிரநான் மறையாளர் நாளும்
முறையால் வணங்கவ் வணங்காய சோதித்
தேவாதி தேவன் திகழ்கின்ற தில்லைத்
திருச்சித்ர கூடம்.

of all the three. Among the works ascribed to him are three ulās, as they are called, pieces of conventional composition celebrating a patron as he passes in triumph through the streets of his capital, appealing to his vanity by elaborate descriptions of the effects produced upon the lady folk of the city. I take the following extracts from the *Kulōttunga-cholanulā* [6] and *Rājarājanulā* [7] regarding the Vishṇu shrine at Chidambaram. These two passages indicate in no uncertain terms that, in carrying out the renovation of the temple, Kulōttunga found the opportunity to get rid of the 'old little gods' which were obnoxious to his piety. That the Vishṇu shrine was what was particularly offensive to this pious

6 புவனி முழுதுடைய பொற்றொடியுந் தானும்
அவனி சுரர்சுருதி யார்ப்ப—நவநிதி தோய்ந்
தேத்தற் கருங்கடவு ளெல்லையிலா னந்தக்
கூத்தைக் களிகூரக் கும்பிட்டுப்—போற்றினமேற்
றில்லைத் திருமன்றின் முன்றிற்—சிறுதெய்வத்
தொல்லைக் குறும்பு தொலைத்தெடுத்து

திருவே திருமாலை

7 சூட்டத் திருமகுடஞ் சூட்டியபின்—ஒட்டு
பொன்னிற் குயிற்றிப் புறம்பிற் குறும்பனைத்து
முன்னிற் கடல்களில் மூழ்குவித்த—சென்னி
திருமகன் ஸ்ரீராஜ ராஜன்

devotee is clear from the expression முன்னிற் கடலில் மூழ்குவித்த, which means 'submerging in the sea, the former house'. This very idea of the author and the same act of his zealous patron find expression in another work, the *Takkayāgapparani.*[8] It is clear then that Kulōttunga II, the grandson of the first of that name, perpetrated this act of pious hostility to the Govindarāja shrine, which led to the establishment by Rāmānuja of the shrine at Tirupati town.

Last of all is a Sanskrit extract which lets us know how the Govindarāja temple came to be again where it is at present. It is a quotation from the *Prapannāmritram* of a certain Anantārya, a descendent of Āndhrapūrṇa who was a contemporary of Rāmānuja. It is a life of Rāmānuja and his followers at the end of which the author of the life gives his own genealogy. In the course of this pedigree occurs

8 முன்றிற் கிடந்த கருங்கடல் போய் முன்னைக்கடல்
[புகப்பின்னைத் தில்லை
மன்றக் கிடங்கண்ட கொண்டல் பெற்ற மரகத
[மேருவை வாழ்த்துவனே—

a passage,[9] which, freely rendered, means that Rāmarāya, who came after Krishnarāya, once went to Chandragiri taking with him his Guru Tatārya. Mahāchārya (Doḍḍayāchārya, as he is popularly called) of the Vādūlagōtra at the height of fame for learning, was then in residence at Ghaṭikāchalam (Sholingar). He wished to restore the temple of Govinda-rāja at Chidambaram (Chitrakūṭa), which had been uprooted by the Chola Krimikanṭa. Overcoming in argument the invincible

9 श्रीरामदेवरायाख्यः कृष्णरायादनन्तरम् ।
शशास राज्यं धर्मेण गुरुभक्तिपरायणः ॥
सभूपतिर्महातेजा ययौ चन्द्रगिरिं प्रति ।
गुरुं ताताख्यामादाय रामरायाभिधस्तदा ॥
तस्मिन्काले महाचार्य सर्व शास्त्रविदां वरः
अवर्तताप्रतिद्वन्द्वो वाधूलो घटिकाचले ॥
किलीकृतं चित्रकूटं क्रिमिकण्ठेन यत्पुरा ।
तत्प्रतिष्ठापितुं सम्यक् तदा मेने महागुरुः ॥
रामरायसहायेन महाचार्यो महायशाः ।
दुर्जयानपी निर्जित्य शैवां शास्त्रविदुत्तमः ॥
स सम्यक् स्थापयामास गोविन्दं चित्रकूटके ॥
गोविंदराजो भगवान् महाचार्यप्रतिष्ठितः ।
महोच्छ्रयश्चित्रकूटे ह्यद्यापि परिदृश्यते ॥

Śaivas, this great one in learning restored the Govindaraja temple at Chitrakūṭa with the assistance of Ramarāya. This Govindarāja thus established by Mahācharya is even yet to be seen at Chidambaram.

These are isolated facts gathered from a number of works, showing no obvious connexion with each other. How are they to be brought together and used to serve the purposes of history ?

The first essential to history is chronology. If the facts are not placed in the order in which I have placed them, they will be unintelligible; and to place them in this order more is required than mere individual ingenuity. If the last fact of the above series could only be placed before its predecessor, the contention of the recent litigants would find some justification. Unfortunately, however, for them I am not marshalling here facts in law for a judge and jury, but facts of history for a critical student. The investigation of the historian ought first of all to be chronological.

The date of Māṇikkavāśagar cannot yet be regarded as a settled fact of history. Varying dates are ascribed to him, as often with as without evidence. Some refer him to the fifth century A.D.; others to the ninth century; others again to an antiquity not definitely ascertainable. That Sundaramūrtināyanār does not include him among the Tiruttoṇḍar is one fact all are agreed upon; and that he was a contemporary of a Varaguṇapāṇḍyan is also tradition accepted on all hands. The epigraphist would keep him to the Varaguṇa of the eighth century after Christ. The literary critic sees quotations and adaptation from Māṇikkavāśagar in the works of the earlier aḍiyārs of the Śaiva hagiology. That his works were well known in the thirteenth century, and the work that readily challenged comparison with those of Māṇikkavāśagar was the Tiruvoymoḷi of Nammāḷvār are in evidence in the following lines[10] of the *Saṭagoparandādi*,

10 துறவா தவர்க்குந் துறந்தவர்க் குஞ்சொல்லவே சுரக்கும்
அறவா விலையிங் கோராயிரம் நிற்கவந் தோரிலர்போய்
மறவா தியர்சொன்ன வாசக மாமலட் டாலைவப்பற்றிக்
கறவாக் கிடப்பரங் கென்பெற வோதங்கள் லைவிப்பே—

ascribed to Kamban, who, there are good reasons for believing, lived in the twelfth century A.D.

In this, as is evident, Kamban compares the thousand of Nammāḻvār to a thousand milch-cows, both to the renounced and to the worldly; and the *Tiruvaśagam* to cows which give no milk. We are not concerned with the judgment here, but only with the fact of the case, although it must be said in passing that this prince of poets in Tamil is far from being a fanatical sectarian; for he says in the *Ramayana*,[11] 'it is impossible to attain salvation for those who dispute in ignorance that Hara is the greater or the world measuring Hari.'

Regarding the two Āḻvārs the dates are no more fixed than for Māṇikkavāśagar. They are both of them anterior to the middle of the eleventh century A.D., inscriptions of which date refer to the works of these Āḻvārs as

11 அரனதிக னுலகளந்த வரியதிகன் எனவுரைக்கு [மறிவி லார்க்குப்
பரகதிசென் றடைவரிய பரிசேபோல்

having been held in high esteem. One [12] of the decades of Tirumangaiāḻvār refers to the occupation of Kanchi by a king called Vairamēghan in the following terms. The first being, that is in Aṭṭabhuyagaram in Kanchi, that was surrounded by the forces and fame of Vairamēghan of long garland and high crown, entitled to the respectful submission of the Pallava, the ruler of the Tondas (people of Tondamandalam). It is often not noticed that two distinct personages are under reference : the ruler of Kānchi (Tondayarkon)—and another entitled to his allegiance, called *Vairamēghan*. This last is in all likelihood the Rāshṭrakuta king of the name, and not Dantivarman Pallava, the son of Nandivarman Pallavamalla.

The only date so far known for Vairamēgha Dantidurga of the Rāshṭrakūṭa dynasty is A. D. 754. The latter half of the eighth century A. D. may, therefore, be taken as the age of Tirumangaiāḻvār.[13] The earlier

12 மன்னவன் றொண்டையர்கோன் வணங்குநீள்
[முடிமாலை வயிரமேகன்
தன்வலிதன் புகழ்சூழ்ந்தகச்சியட்ட புயகரத்தாதி —

13 *Vide* Chapter XIX of the author's Ancient India.

quotations would then refer us to the eighth and ninth centuries A. D. at the latest for the existence of the Govindarāja temple at Chidambaram.

The next batch of references leads to the inference that it was Kulōttunga II, the son of Vikramachola and the father of Rājarāja II A.D. (*circa*) 1133 to 1150, who uprooted the shrine in his pious work of renovation of the great Śaiva temple. This is clear from the quotations themselves which are from the works of a contemporary author.

Lastly, the Sanskrit quotation refers the reconstruction to Doḍḍayācharya through the good offices of a Rāmarāja who ruled after Krishnarāya. It was in this connetion that this teacher (āchārya) came in contact with Appaiya Dikshita, the great South Indian scholar and philosopher. In his commentary on Vēdānta Dēsika's *Yādavābhyudayam*, this scholar says that he took up the work of a commentary on this kāvya at the instance of Pinna Timma, grandson of Rāmarāja. The Rāmarāja referred to is clearly the one that fell at Talikōta. There is nothing very improbable in Appaiya Dikshita's having been contemporaneous with Doḍḍayācharya or Rāmarāja on the one hand, and with Pinna Timmarāya on the other. Besides the writer of the *Prapannāmrtam* itself was a disciple of Kumāratātārya, popularly Koṭikanyakādānam Tātāchar, whose patron was Vankaṭapatirāya, who ruled till A.D. 1614. It must therefore be sometime before A.D. 1565 that the temple was restored.

We are thus able to obtain an account of the vicissitudes of this temple for about five centuries at least. I have taken this as a simple illustration of what historical information can be gained even from apparently unconnected literature. The facts here are all the more reliable, even including the last, as they are mere incidental references. It will now appear that there can be no history without chronology, and the attempts to fix the dates of works and authors, which to many appear absurd, is of the essence of historical research.

What is wanted, therefore, now for historical research is a systematic and organized study of literature, both vernacular and Sanskrit, in a way that will facilitate work both literary and historical. This work cannot be done by one man all through for his own requirements. He will require the collaboration of a number of others. A student engaged in historical research has to keep himself in close touch with the archæological, epigraphical and literary work that may be going on, and must be something of an archæologist and epigraphist himself; but that any one should be all the three by himself is beyond human possibility in most cases. This is very often recognized, and the two branches are held to be distinct. In point of literature also—I am concerned with literature only as an auxiliary to history—the collection of manuscripts and documents, and the bringing out of good and critical editions of works ought to be regarded as quite a distinct branch. Most editions of the classics published in India till quite recently, both in Sanskrit and the vernaculars, were uncritical editions. It is the Bombay Sanskrit Series, that set the fashion for Sanskrit. Our esteemed countryman, Mahāmahōpādyaya Swaminatha Aiyar, has given us a number of remarkably well-edited texts of important Tamil works. The advantages of this kind of editing are quite apparent. The various readings are given for the reader to choose from; the variety of comments are also noted. When this is well and accurately done the text editor has rendered good service to the historian. What then is the utility of such editions? To give only an example or two. The learned editor of the *Śilappadhikāram*, Pundit Swaminatha Aiyar, has taken care to give in a footnote thirteen lines at the beginning of the second canto, found only in one manuscript among those he consulted. He remarks in another place that manuscripts found in the same quarter have been the most reliable in many particulars. These thirteen lines refer to Karikāla as the ruler at the time, and state that the *Paṭṭinappālai* had been dedicated to him by the author, thus confirming the inferable contemporaneity of this ruler with the author of the work. There are references to the same incident in other works but far later in point of time.

Similarly in stanza fourteen of Kāḷidāsa's *Mēghadūta*, where there is the reference to Dinnāga, it struck me that the interpretation of the whole, as applied to Dinnāgāchārya, was forced ; for in the alternative interpretation the commentator Mallinātha has to omit a part of a compound word. The pundits whom I consulted consider that that is no bar to the slēsha (double entendre). I understand now from a Bombay edition of the text and commentary that Hēmādri does not countenance the interpretation. The result is that the estimate of Kāḷidāsa's age, based on his contemporaneity with Dinnāga, falls to the ground so far. Hēmādri may be right or Mallinātha ; but he who reads with a view to building up a hypothesis in history ought to have an opportunity of knowing both the commentaries. Then he formulates his hypothesis at his own risk.

Further down Mallinātha lays down that the three ślokas which he comments on are interpolations. He does not choose to tell us why he thinks so, though his reasons would have been valuable. There is a great and important amount of work to be done, in the way of examining critically the texts with a view to distinguish the genuine from the spurious part of it.

It is alleged, often with truth, that the historian reads his thoughts and feelings into the writings of the past. This no doubt is a defect that he has to guard himself against. If the record of the past is placed in his hands in an accurate form he ought to have no excuse for making such mistakes. The defect arises from an insufficiency of information which would enable him to form a complete idea of the men and of the period he is dealing with. This is a point that the late Professor Maitland seems to have laid great stress on in the course of his lectures. It is in regard to oaths and the influence that they exercised on truthfulness of the witness that the Professor took occasion to make the remark. This defective appreciation is considerably in evidence among a class of scholars engaged in research work. It is traceable to the importing of our own ideas and the circumstances about us to periods of which we have either no, or have no means of having, full information. To illustrate the position I go back to the Bṛhatkathā. The work was written in Paiśāchi and appears to have been held in high esteem by successive writers of note in Sanskrit literature, at least from the days of Daṇḍi to the age of the Kāsmirian Sōmadēva. We have four different versions of it as our only source of knowledge of the work. The *Kathāsarithsāgara* of Sōmadēva, is professedly a translation; Bṛhatkathāmanjari is a collection of stories from the Bṛhatkathā; a third version or collection was obtained from Nepal; and lastly a Tamil translation of it, which is of an antiquity which may be prior to that of the now known Śangam works. Professor Speyer, a Dutch scholar, who has made a critical study of the *Kathāsarithsāgara* has, on the strength of the supernatural powers ascribed to Nāgārjuna in the work, referred the Bṛhatkathā to a period between the third and the fifth century A. D. This is because the Professor thinks that people would hardly have believed in supernatural power unless a considerable interval had elapsed. The inference would certainly be warranted, if all people were rational and sceptical to an equal degree at all periods of history. All the world over, and in regard to all religions, miracles play an important part at a particular stage of development; and people are not wanting in the enlightened twentieth century who have full faith in occultism and spiritualism. This it is that makes several Indian works seem ridiculously absurd to European scholars. If they could appreciate the influence a belief in transmigration exerts upon the minds of simple people, and how closely interwoven it is in all the varying belief of the people in India, they would see that what strikes them as absurd is quite obviously believable even by contemporaries. That this has, as a matter of course, been the case could be proved, if Tamil literature and literary tradition were called into requisition.

There are several works in Tamil called mahākāvyas. The translation of the Bṛhatkathā, a śirukāppyam or a minor kāvya called *Udayanan kadai* or *Peruṇgadai* or even simply *kadai*, is believed to be the work which gave the authority for the use of the word kāvya. This work is ascribed to the period of the middle Śaṉgam, that is, anterior to the third Śaṉgam, the works of which we have in some number. I have put forward my arguments for referring the third Śangam to the earlier centuries of the Christian era; hence this work ought to be referable to a period coeval with the beginning of the era of Christ. If only this could be established beyond a doubt, the history of Vikramāditya and Kanishka, about which there is yet considerable divergence of scholarly opinion, would become settled to a degree not dreamt of by any yet; because, Sōmadēva, the translator of the Bṛhatkathā, says in so many clear words that he makes no change in the matter of the original beyond the mere change of language and the necessary abbreviation. It would be hyper-criticism to dispute the assertion of the author without establishing a clear motive as an essential pre-requisite. This consideration has not always been conceded to him.

There is work to be done, therefore, in the

co-ordination of the study of the two languages, Sanskrit and Tamil, in the interest of both. In the absence of the original, if the Sanskrit translation could be collated and compared with the Tamil, the result would go far towards solving one of the most important problems of ancient Indian History; namely, the origin of the Samvat era which has had to be accounted for in so many fanciful ways by great scholars. There are references in both the *Kathāsarithsāgara* and the Bṛhatkathāmanjari to a Vikramāditya-Vishamaśila, who got rid of the Mlēcha trouble, and came to be regarded an incarnation of the divine energy of Vishṇu or Śiva, it does not matter which to us. This question is too long for discussion here.

My object is not to settle disputed questions or to formulate a new historical hypothesis. Now that archæological and epigraphical work have made some advance, I appeal for a better, more rational, and systematic study of the literature of the country, with a view to making them yield the results that they are capable of. Inscriptions and archæological research can after all provide the dry bones only. All else will have to be got from literature. Besides, there is a period to which inscriptions do not lead us. For such periods we have to depend upon literary evidence alone, if this is available, either from Sanskrit or the vernaculars. It is a duty that every one owes to his country to do all in his power to advance the study of this literature. In addition to the discharging of a duty, this study of literature will be a source of pleasure even to busy people. Here individual effort can take us only a small way. But if these efforts were made to flow into one channel, the volume would be the greater and the work turned out the larger.

CHAPTER I.

SOUTH INDIA A DISTINCT ENTITY IN INDIAN HISTORY.

THE term South India as a distinct expression referring to the southernmost portion of our country, India, goes back to the days of the Mahābhārata in its present form, for its authority. That distinction it has maintained all through historical times even down to the present. The whole of India north of the Vindhya Mountains roughly is what is now known as Hindustan, and was perhaps in olden times included in the expression Uttarāpatha. In days when perhaps the geographical knowledge of India south of the Vindhyas was somewhat vague, the term Dakshiṇāpatha seems to have indicated all the country south of the Vindhyas. But by the time of the compilation of the Mahābhārata in its present form, Dakshiṇāpatha seems to be limited to what we now unnderstand by the term Dekhan.

Sahadeva in his southern expedition before the celebration of the Rājasūya (a sacrifice celebrated in token of paramount power) by his eldest brother, conquered the Puḷindas, marched southwards from them into the Pāndya country. After fighting a successful battle against the Pāndyas, he moved northwards towards the Dakshiṇāpatha.[1] The first

[1] Mahābhārata Kumbh. Ed.

तांस्तानाटविकान् सर्वानजयत् पाण्डुनन्दनः ।
वाताधिपं च नृपतिं वशे चक्रेमहाबलः ॥ १६ ॥
पुलिंदांश्च रणे जित्वा ययौ दक्षिणतः पुरः ।
युयुधे पाण्ड्यराजेन दिवसं नकुलानुजः ॥ १७ ॥
तं जित्वा स महा बाहुः प्रययौ दक्षिणापथम् ।
गुहामासादयामास किष्किन्धां लोक विश्रुताम् ॥ १८ ॥

* * *

गच्छ पाण्डवशार्दूल रत्नान्यादाय सर्वशः ।
अविघ्नमस्तु कार्याय धर्मराजाय धीमते ॥ २२ ॥
ततो रत्नान्युपादाय पुरीं माहिष्मतीं ययौ ।
तत्र नीलेन राज्ञा स चक्रे युद्धं नरर्षभः ॥ २३ ॥

(Mahābhārata II. 32. Sl. 16-23.) (See also Sl. 70-76)

state that he went to on this frontier was Kishkinda, (the modern Hampi). The next state that he came to was Māhishmati (Māndhāta on the Narmada river).

Similarly in the Rāmāyana,[2] Sugriva

2 सहस्र शिरसं विन्ध्यं नानाद्रुमलतायुतम् ।
नर्मदां च नदीं दुर्गां महोरगनिषेविताम् ॥ ८ ॥
ततो गोदावरीं रम्यां कृष्णवेणीं महानदीम् ।
वरदां च महाभागां महोरगनिषेविताम् ॥ ९ ॥
मेखलामुत्कलां चैव दशार्णनगराण्यपि ।
अश्ववन्तीमवन्तीं च सर्वमेवानुपश्यत ॥ १० ॥
विदर्भानृषिकांश्चैव रम्यान्माहिषकानपि ।

Rishikān in the text is an obvious error for Rishṭikān.

तथा वंगान्कलिङ्गांश्च कौशिकांश्च समन्ततः ॥ ११ ॥
अन्वीक्ष्य दण्डकारण्यं सपर्वतनदीगुहम् ।
नदीं गोदावरीं चैव सर्वमेवानुपश्यत ।
तथैवान्ध्रांश्च पुण्ड्रांश्च चोलान्पाण्ड्यान्सकेरलान् ॥ १२ ॥

* * *

ततस्तामापगां दिव्यां प्रसन्नसलिलां शिवाम् ।
तत्र द्रक्ष्यथ कावेरीं विहितामप्सरोगणैः ॥ १५ ॥
तस्यासीनां नगस्याग्रे मलयस्य महौजसम् ।
द्रक्ष्यथादित्यसङ्काशमगस्त्यमृषिसत्तमम् ॥ १६ ॥

directing his search party to the south, gave them the following description of that region, beginning from the centre, the river Śarāvati in the Madyadēśa which flows in a circle and loses itself in the sand. He divides this region obviously into three portions:—the region north of the Daṇḍakāraṇya and in the immediate neighbourhood of the Vindhyas; then the region along the East Coast up to the river Krishna; and then the region south of the Krishna. In the second region on the south of the Vindhyas figured Vidarbha, Rishṭika,

ततस्तेनाभ्यनुज्ञाताः प्रसन्नेन महात्मना ।
ताम्रपर्णीं ग्राहजुषां तरिष्यथ महानदीम् ॥ १७ ॥
सा चन्दनवनैर्दिव्यैः प्रच्छन्ना द्वीपशालिनी ।
कान्तेव युवतिः कान्तं समुद्रमवगाहते ॥ १८ ॥
ततो हेममयं दिव्यं मुक्तामणिविभूषितम् ।
युक्तं कवाटं पाण्ड्यानां गता द्रक्ष्यथ वानराः ॥ १९ ॥
ततः समुद्रमासाद्य संप्रधार्यार्थनिश्चयम् ।
अगस्त्येनान्तरे तत्र सागरे विनिवेशितः ॥ २० ॥
चित्रनानानगः श्रीमान्महेन्द्रः पर्वतोत्तमः ।
जातरूपमयः श्रीमानवगाढो महार्णवम् ॥ २१ ॥

(Vālmīki Rāmāyana III. 41. Sl. 8-21.)

and Māhishaka on the one side, Vanga, Kalinga and Kauśika on the other. Then he puts in the Dandakāranyam in which is included the river Godaveri. Then come in the country of the Andhras, the Puṇḍras, the Cholas, the Pāṇḍyas, the Cheras. Then is given a description of the Kauvery passing on to the hill Malaya, the residence of sage Agastya. Then is described the Tāmravarni river, which they are advised to cross. Then is described the famous place Pāṇḍya Kavāṭam, generally identified with Kavāṭapuram or Kapāṭapuram in Tamil. Then is described the hill Mahēndra across the sea in an island. The older Puranas such as the Matsya,[3] Vāyu,[4] and even Mārkaṇḍēya are not perhaps so clear in respect of the distinction between the two parts of the region south of the Vindhyas, but they give the main divisions practically along the same lines.

In respect of these works, however, it would be impossible to make anything like a chrono-

3 Ch. 104 Anandāśrama Edn.

4 XLV sl. 70 onwards to the *end* the same edition as the above.

logical inference, though it may now be taken as agreed that both the works, the Mahābhārata and the Rāmāyana may have to be referred to the fifth century B. C. It still is a matter of great doubt as to what exactly is the age of any particular part of the work. In this respect, the Rāmāyana, stands somewhat on a better footing than the Mahābhārata, and a statement made in respect of any book or chapter of these works can be challenged in respect of any chronological datum. Hence while the occurrence of the names of the divisions stated above is a matter of some importance, the references do not enable us exactly to fix the period to which the division would have reference. We may state roughly, however, that these were probably divisions definitely formed and familiarly recognised in the fourth century before Christ.

Another class of literary sources which can be exploited for the purpose is the Buddhist Jātakas and Buddhist literature generally. The countries in India which figure among them have reference to about sixteen kingdoms and a few tribal republics. Arranging them on the map, the southernmost portion reached is perhaps Paiṭān on the Godavery in the western extremity, Aśmaka[5] being the only southern kingdom referred to there at all. The earliest available Buddhist literature therefore does not take us very much beyond the Vindhya mountains, and that seems reflected in one benedictory verse, which occurs at the end of several of the dramas of Bhāsa. The verse merely refers to a wish 'may our Rājasimha bring the whole of the earth from sea to sea, and from the Vindhyas to the Himalayas under one umbrella, and rule it with success.[6]

Passing on now to another class of Sanskrit works which can be dated closer than these, the researches of Sir R. G. Bhandarkar show that to the Grammarian Pāṇini the south was a land unknown. The countries farthest to the south mentioned by him are Kachcha,

5 The Mahābhārata in another place refers to Aśmākī (I. 63. 12) a *Yādhava princess* married to Prāchinvan This would indicate the upper reaches of the Godaveri as at least one Aśmaka.

6 इमां सागर पर्यन्तां हिमवन् विन्ध्यकुण्डलाम् ।
महीं एकाथपत्राङ्कां राजसिंहः प्रशास्तुनः ॥

Avanti, Kosala, Karūśa and Kalinga.[7] None of these takes us south of the Vindhyas. All these are in fact states "on the back of the Vindhyas," according to the Purāṇas. The Vartika on Pāṇini of Kātyāyana who, according to Bhandarkar, followed Pāṇini more than two centuries after, shows considerable acquaintance with the south. Kātyāyana notes the omission by Pāṇini of the name Pāṇḍya and explains it as "one sprung from an individual of the tribe of the Pāṇḍus or the king of their country should be called a Pāṇḍya." Another of Pāṇini's rules is extended by Kātyāyana to apply to the Cholas and others. Coming down to Patanjali, we find a very much more intimate acquaintance in him of the geography of the south. Of the southern places, he mentions Māhishmati, Vidarbha, both of them in the Dekhan and immediately south of the Vindhyas, Kānchipuram and Kērala which take us very near to the extreme south. There is besides the general rule that he laid down that a word like Sarasī is used to denote large lakes in the south; hence it is possible

7 Bombay Gaz. Vol. I, Part 2, p. 138—39.

for us to infer that in Patanjali's time about 150 B. C. the whole of South India was known to the northerners. In the time of Kātyāyana about 350 B. C., South India was fairly well-known while in the days of Pāṇini, according to Sir R. G. Bhandarkar, about the seventh century B. C. South India was practically unknown.

Coming down to more definitely historical works, the following extract from Magasthenes shows at any rate that some knowledge of the Pāndya country had reached him. He says, from hearsay information obviously, that Herakles beget a daughter in India whom he called Pandaia. To her he assigned that portion of India which lies to the southward and extends to the sea while he distributed the people subject to her rule in 365 villages, giving orders that one village each day should bring to the treasury the royal tribute, so that the queen might always have assistance of those men whose turn it was to pay the tribute, in coercing those who for the time being were defaulters in their payment. He was further informed that this female sovereign had an army of 500 elephants, 4,000 cavalry and 130,000 infantry, and possessed great treasure in the fishery for pearls, which according to Arrian were greatly sought by both the Greeks and the Romans.

The Arthaśāstra of Chanakya, referable to the same time as Magasthenes, has two references known to me to the South. Speaking of pearls and their quality, Chanakya refers to Tāmravarṇika "that which is produced in the Tāmravarṇi"; Pāṇḍya Kavāṭaka [6], that which is obtained in Pāṇḍya Kavāṭa. (p. 86 of Mr. Shama Sastry's Trans.)

Further in the same chapter, but speaking this time of cotton fabrics, the Arthaśāstra has

6 This Pāṇḍya Kavāṭa, a door-way of the Pāṇḍyas,' is a fine commentary on the Kavāṭam Pāṇdyānām of the Rāmāyana. The commentator on the Arthaśāstra explains it as a mountain known as Malayakōṭi in the Pāṇḍya country. It is rather of doubtful propriety that a place where pearls are found should be referred to as a mountain. It seems much more likely that the expression Pāṇḍya Kavāṭa means, the door-way of entry into the Pāṇḍya country from the sea and the Malayakōṭi of the commentator therefore, would then be the promontory where the Western Ghats dips into the sea.

reference to the fabrics of Madhura, which the commentator explains rightly as southern Madura, and it may be noted also that among other places remarkable for cotton fabrics figures Kalinga, the Tamil name for cloth generally being Kalingam. (p. 94, *Ibid*).

Next in order of time, the edicts of Asoka do specifically mention the southern kingdoms, and place them as beyond the imperial pale of the Mauryan Empire. Three of his rock edicts mention these, and they are edicts II, V, and XIII.

II. 'Everywhere in the empire of King Priyadarśin, beloved of the gods, as well as among those nations and princes that are *his neighbours, such as the Choḍas*, the *Pamḍiyas*, the *Satiyaputra*, the *Keralaputa*; *Tambapamni*, the Yona king, called *Amtiyoka* as well as among those who are the *vassal-kings of that Amtiyoka*, everywhere king Priyadarśin, beloved of the gods, has founded two (2) kinds of hospitals, both hospitals, for men and hospitals for animals. Everywhere where herbs wholesome for men and wholesome for animals are not found, they have been imported and sown by the king's order. And wells have been dug by his order for the enjoyment of men and beasts.'

V. 'Now a long period has passed, and the officials called the Overseers of the Sacred Law have formerly not existed. Now, when I had been anointed thirteen years, I appointed Overseers of the Sacred Law. They are busy among all sects with watching over the sacred law, with the growth of the law, and with the welfare and happiness of my loyal subjects, as also among the *Yonas*, *Kamboyas*, *Gamdharas*, *Rishṭikas*, *Piṭinikas* and *all other nations which are my neighbours.*'

XIII. 'But this conquest the beloved of the gods holds the chiefest, *viz.*, the conquest through the Sacred Law. And that conquest had been made by the Beloved of the gods both here *in his empire*, and over all *his neighbours*, even as far as six hundred yojanas, where the king of the Yonas, called *Amtiyoka* dwells, and beyond this Amtiyoka, where the *four* (4) *Kings* dwell, *viz.*, he called *Turamaya*, he called *Amtikini*, he called *Maka*, and he called *Alikasudara**; further in the south, where the *Choḍas* and *Pamḍas* dwell as far as *Tambapamni*; likewise where the king dwells, among the Viśas, Vajris, the Amdhras, and Pulidas everywhere they follow the teaching of the Beloved of the gods with respect to the Sacred Law. Even those to whom the messengers of the Beloved of the gods do not go, follow the Sacred Law, as soon as they have heard of the orders of the

*(1) Antiochus, Theos, of Asia, 261—246 B.C.
(2) Ptoleny II Philadelphia, 285—247 B.C.
(3) Antigonus Gonatas, 278—239 B.C.
(4) Magas of Cyrene, d. 258 B.C.
(5) Alexander of Epirus, 272—? 258 B.C.

Beloved of the gods, issued in accordance with the Sacred Law, and his teaching of the Sacred Law, and they will follow it in future.' (Buhler in Epigraphia Indica II).

These edicts, it will be seen, refer to a number of rulers and by implication to the regions over which they ruled. They seem also to be classified into two groups: those that are his neighbours and perhaps in a position of subordination to him, and those with whom his relations were on terms of independence and equality. Among the former have to be included the Yonas, Kambojas, the Gandharas, all of them along the north-western frontier. The Yonas, must have been the Greek state of Bactria and the subordinate chieftaincies thrown out from there perhaps in the Kabul Valley and elsewhere, where they might have spread out. The Kambhojas are usually located in the north-western corner of Kashmir extending downwards. The Gandharas were the people in the region westward of the Punjab, including the two capitals Taxila and Pushkalāvati, that is the region between Kabul and India along the Kaibar way. The other two regions mentioned are the Rashṭikas and Pitenikas. The Rishṭikas perhaps were a vast group of people among whom Mahrattas were the principal group, there being other Rashṭikas or Rishtikas besides. There is nothing to connect them with the Āraṭṭas, but the Saurāshṭras or the name Surāshṭra for the country may be originally traceable to them. It is a little more doubtful if the same could be said of Gūrjarāshṭra (Gujarat) and Piṭenikas,[9] the country round about Paiṭan on the Godaveri.

We are justified by edict II quoted above, in distinguishing the empire of King Pryadarśin and his neighbours the independent monarchs, such as the Chola, the Pāṇḍya, the Satīyaputra and Kēraḷaputra in the south, and Amtiyoka (Amtiyoks) and his vassal-kings in the west. In regard to these southern monarchs the Cholas, the Pāṇḍyas, and the Kēraḷa are plain enough to us. They are respectively the coast country on the east extending per-

9 The form Paiṭān from Prathishtāna is considered unsound philologically. Sans. Prithishtāna, becoming Patiṭṭana thro: Payiṭṭana into Piṭṭaṇa seems possible as a folk etymology or apabhramśa philology even.

haps from the Pulikat to the Vellar in the Pudukotta State with its capital at Uraiyūr. The Pāṇḍya country next following extending from coast to coast along a line drawn from perhaps the point Kalimere to Koṭṭayam, with its capital at Madura, and the Kērala country along the western coast, extending northwards of this, and including in it the northern half of Travancore, the State of Cochin and considerable portions of Malabar. The Satiya-putra seems obviously to refer to the region immediately north of this and the name Satiyaputra seems normally to indicate the prevalence of the Matriarchate or Aḷiyasantānam Law. These are put on a level with the Greek King Antiochus. Theos (God), grandson of Seleucus Nicator (Victorious) the rival and friend of Chandragupta. This edict makes the position clear so far that these states were beyond the boundaries of the empire of Asoka.

Coming down to edict V, which relates to the appointment of Overseers of the Sacred Law, Asoka distinguishes between "My loyal subjects and those among the Yonas and other people, and then all other nations his neighbours," which seems to indicate that the Yonas and the other people were in some sense subordinate to him perhaps tributary states under him. The Edict XIII on the contrary makes the division between his empire and all his neighbours, and again puts Aṁtiyoka and his four neighbours on a footing similar to the Cholas and their neighbours the Pāṇḍyas. He makes the further distinction of those to whom the "Messengers of the Beloved of the Gods" are sent, and those to whom they do not go. The best commentary upon this arrangement of his is in the Mahāvamśa of Ceylon where we find the following:

"When the Thera Moggaliputta, the illuminator of the religion of the Conqueror, had brought the (third) council to an end and when, looking into the future, he had beheld the founding of the religion in adjacent countries, (then) in the month Kattika he sent forth theras, one here and one there. The thera Majjhantika he sent to Kashmira and Gandhāra, the thera Mahādēva he sent to Mahishamaṇḍala. To Vanavāsa he sent the thera named Rakkhita, and to Aparāntaka the Yona named Dhammarakkhita; to Mahaāṭṭha (he sent) the thera named Mahādhammarakk hita, but the thera Mahārakkhita he sent into the country of the Yona. He sent the thera Majjhima to the Himalaya country, and to Suvaṇṇabhūmi he sent the two theras Śoṇa and Uttara. The great thera Mahinda, the theras Itthiya, Uttiya, Sambala and Bhaddasala his disciples, these five theras he sent forth with the charge: 'Ye shall found in the lovely island of Lanka the lovely religion of the Conqueror.'" (Geiger's Mahāvaṃśa p. 82).

The passage refers to the missions for the propogation of the faith sent under the command of Asoka to various localities for the purpose of carrying the teachings of the 'Enlightened One' to those regions. Among the territories mentioned here are Kashmir, and Gāndhāra in neighbourhood. Then the next mission was that sent to Mahishamanḍala, which in this case may have to be identified with Māhishmati, though the name Mahishamanḍala is of equal application to the territory which is now Mysore, as will be shown later. The next region is Vanavāsa, which is the Banavasi, 12,000 district in the southern Mahratta country and Mysore. Then comes the region of the northern Konkan coast and that is Aparānta. Then comes Mahārāshṭra; then comes the country of the Yona, which probably was the region somewhere in the immediate neighbourhood of India, Afghanistan or Beluchistan. Then comes the country called Suvarṇabhumi, which is usually identified with the gold-producing province of the Malaya Peninsula and Tennassarim (the Chryse of the classical writers); last and most important of all Ceylon, because it is the history of Buddhism in Ceylon that is the subject of the treatise. This enumeration of countries seems to go so far only to confirm our classifications of the territories referred to in the Asoka edicts as(1)those of his empire proper, (2) of the dependencies of the empire and (3) of states in independent diplomatic relations. If the Māhishamanḍala referred to here stands for the country of the Māhishakas round Māndhāta, on the Narbada, for which there is very good reason, then Banavasi is the southernmost limit, and we find India south of the fourteenth degree of latitude out of the pale of imperial rule.

This is confirmed in another way though somewhat less directly from the Mahāvaṃśa itself. Duṭṭagāmaṇi Abhaya on the occasion of laying the foundation-stone of the great Stūpa (Thūpa) had called for an assembly of most of the leading Buddhists from the various Buddhist centres. In response to this invitation there assembled :—

			Bhikhus from
1	Indagutta	with 80,000 ,,	Rājagāha (Rajagraha capital of Maghada).
2	Dhammasēna	,, 12,000 ,,	Iśipaṭana (the Deer-Park in Benares.
3	Piyadassi	,, 60,000 ,,	Jētārāma-vibara(Vibara outside of Śrāvasti in Nepal Tharai.)
4	Urubuddharakkbite	,, 80,000 ,,	Mahāvana (in Vaiśāli.)
5	Urudhammarakkhita	,, 30,000 ,,	Ghōsitārāma (In Kośambi)
6	Urusamgharakkhita	,, 40,000 ,,	Dakkhiṇagira-vibara in Ujjeni (Ujjain in Malva.)
7	Mittiṇṇa	,, 160,000 ,,	Aśokārāma in Pupphapura (Pāṭaliputra or Patna.)
8	Uttiṇṇa	,, 280,000 ,,	Kashmir.

9 Mahādēva	„ 460,000 „		Pallavabhogga (the Fief of the Pallavas probably in Gujarat, also regions of the Indus).
10 Yonamahādhammarakkhita	„ 30,000 „		Alasanda, the city of the Yonas, Alexandria of the Yonas which may be one of the many Alexandrias, Alexandria near Kabul, Alexandria near the junction of the Jhelum and the Indus or Karachi, which was itself one of the Alexandrias.
11 Uttara	„ 60,000 „		Road of the Vindhyan forests.
12 Chittagupta	„ 30,000 „		Bodhimaṇḍa-vihara (in Bodhgaya).
13 Chandagupta	„ 80,000 „		Vanavāsa country (Banavasi in the Dharwar dist.)
14 Suriyagutta	„ 96,000 „		Great Kēlasa-vihara probably Kailasa-vihara which may be from the region of Ellora in the present Nizam's dominions, or Amarāvati, Guntur.

(Opuscoli pp. 193, 194.)

Here again it will be noticed that the famous Buddhist centres do not come beyond Vanavāsa, and this has reference to the period A.B. 382 to 406, or 101 to 77 B.C. on the basis of B.C. 483 for Buddha Nirvana.

This position is confirmed by what we can derive from early Tamil literature but before passing on to that, we may say a word about this Ceylon chronicle. This is a chronicle of the history of Buddhism maintained in one of the many monasteries of the Buddhists, and was put together in its present form in the sixth century A. D. by the Sthavira monk, Mahānāman. That was done obviously in commentary upon the earlier, but somewhat less classical Dipavamśa which was composed in the fourth century A. D. as it stops short in its account with the reign of Mahāsēna, who came to the throne sometime about A. D. 306. Even this Dipavamśa is believed to have derived its material from various Aṭṭakathas (Sans. Arthakathā, stories in exposition of the meaning of various portions of the Buddhist gospel). Thus while it is possible that the reference has contemporaneous authority, we could have little doubt that it belongs at any rate to the fourth century A. D., if not earlier. This fourth century authority goes only to confirm what is indicated in the edicts and what perhaps is unconsciously expounded in early Tamil literature. We shall pass on to this last now.

CHAPTER II.

MAURYAN INVASION OF SOUTH INDIA.

TILL recently it was held doubtful that the references to the Chola, Pāṇḍya and Kēraḷa in Asoka's edicts, had anything more in them than a mere boast on the part of the Buddhist Emperor. The discovery of his edicts at Siddhāpura, Brahmagiri and Jaṭinga Rāmesvara hill in Mysore in 1892 did put the edicts upon a somewhat better footing in respect of their veracity. The discovery two years ago of a copy of Asoka's edicts in Maski, in the Nizam's dominions, gave new and powerful support to the contention of those that maintained that Asoka's territory actually extended to the frontiers of Mysore. This last discovery is of the highest historical value, as the edicts are almost a replica of those at Sāhasram and therefore of a time somewhere about his thirteenth year.[1] The Mysore edicts seem later. If then, as the

[1] Hyderabad Archælogical Series: No. 1. p. 3.

Maski edicts shew, there was a southern province of Asoka, and if the Suvarnnagiri, the capital of the Aryaputta and the Mahamatras, has to be looked for round Maski itself or in the territory of the Ancient Kuntala, [2] when was South India conquered and how far did the conquest go actually? Light is shed upon this darkness from an unexpected source, and that is, classical Tamil Literature.

Before proceeding to let this light in, it is necessary to know what exactly is the present position of historians in regard to this matter. Mr. Vincent A. Smith in his Early History of India (Third Edition), which is later than his monograph on Asoka, has on page 163 "The Tamil States extending to the extremity of the Peninsula, and known as the Chola and Pāṇḍya kingdoms, certainly were independent as were the Kērḷaputra and Satiyaputra states on the south-western, or Malabar Coast. The southern frontier of the empire may be described approximately as a line drawn from the mouth of the Pennar River, near Nellore on

2 Para. 1. *Ibid.*

the Eastern coast through Cuddappah and to the south of Chitaldroog (North. lat. 14 13', F. Long. 76 24) to the river Kalyānapuri on the west coast (about N. Lat. 14), which forms the northern boundary of the Tuḷuva country, probably representing the old kingdom of Satiyaputra." In regard to this southern boundary the limits marked out in the extract are substantially correct on the information furnished by epigraphy. This correctness is confirmed by what we are able to glean from Tamil literary sources except in regard to the eastern limit of this line. The Tamils marked out the limit of Tamil land at Pulikat, which is the Anglo-Indian corruption of Paḻavērkkāḍu (old forest of Vēl. trees). [3] This is referred to in Ancient Tamil literature as Vērkkāḍu, without the adjective for 'old' standing before the name. This

3 குல்லைக் கண்ணி வடுகர் முனையது
வல்வேற் காட்டினன் னாட்டும்பர்
மொழிபெயர் தேஎத்த ராயினும்
வழிவிடல் சூழ்ந்திசி னவருடை நாட்டே.

Māmūlar in Kurumtokai 11.

is usually described as Vaḍukarmunai, the end of the Northerners' territory. When this limit is passed the language also changes (Moḻipeyartēm,[4] the country where the spoken language changes to another). The limit on the other side is given as the Tuḷu land or Koṇkānam [5], the territory of the chief Nannan in the first century of the Christian era, which

4 பனிபடு சோலை வேங்கடத் தும்பர்
மொழி பெயர்தே எத்தரென்ப.

Māmulanār in Aham. 210/11.

வென்றியோடு
வில்லலைத்துண்ணும் வல்லாண் வாழ்க்கை
தமிழ்கெழு மூவர் காக்கும்
மொழி பெயாதே எத்தபன்மலை யிறந்தே

Māmaḷanār in *Ibid* 31.

5 Aham 15. & Naṟṟiṇai 391.

மெய்ம்மலி பெரும்பூட் செம்மற் கோசர்
கொம்மையம் பசுங்காய்க் குடுமி விளைந்த
பாகலார் கைப் பறைக் கட்பீலித்
தோகை காவிற்றுளு நாட்டன்ன.

Aham. 15. Māmūlanār

பொன்படு கொண்கான நன்ன னன்னாட்
டேழிற் குன்றம் பெறினும் பொருள்வயின்
யாரோ பிரிகிற் பவரே.

Naṟṟiṇai 391. Pālaipāḍiya Perungaḍungō.

was broken into by a new people Kōśar, as a result of a war in which Nannan obviously suffered defeat, and lost his state elephant.[6] Thus then, Tamil literature ascribable to about the first century of the Christian era supports the statement that this line constituted the southern boundary of the Mauryas except for a difference of half a degree in the eastern end.

The Dekhan, or Peninsular India, down to approximately the latitude of Nellore, must therefore apparently have been subjugated by either Chandragupta or Bindusāra, because it was inherited from the latter by Asoka, whose only recorded war was the conquest of Kalinga; and it is more probable that the conquest of the south was the work of Bindusara than it was effected by his busy father.' Mr. Vincent A. Smith also notes that the Tibetan historian Tārānātha (Scheifner p. 89) attributes to Bindusāra and Chanakya the conquest of the country between the eastern and western seas.

6 நன்ன
னறுமாகொன்று நாட்டிற் போக்கிய
வொன்றுமொழிக் கோசர் போல.

Paranar in Kuruntogai 73.

The fact of the conquest of the south has remained so far an inference and no more. In regard to the question which of the first three Mauryas did actually make the conquest there is no further direct information than the inference we are left to make from the known extent of Asoka's Empire and the statement of Tārānātha regarding Bindusāra's conquest, unless the last two lines quoted by Dr. Fleet from the Mahāvamśa be held to imply Asoka's conquest [7] of the south.

Among the poets who constituted, according to tradition, the famous third Academy at Madura we find the name Māmulanār, a Brahman scholar whose name, as an author, is held in very high esteem in the Tamil world

7 पत्वा चतुहि वस्सेहि येकरज्जं महायसो ।
पुरे पाटलिपुत्तस्मिन् अत्ताणं अभिसेचयि ॥

(J. R. A. S. 1909. p. 29).

Having attained the sole sovereignty in four years of the first line need not have exclusive reference to the slaughter of his brothers if such could be held to be a historical fact. As a matter of fact it is very doubtful if the massacre of the brothers is at all a fact as rock edict V (Vincent A. Smith's Asoka, p. 162, note 4) refers to his brothers and sisters.

even now His works were of the character of fugitive poems which are found scattered in various collections, all of them generally regarded as having had the 'Śangam (Academy) imprimatur. Without basing his antiquity upon the fact, that his works are found included in these collections, there is enough internal evidence to show that he was an elder contemporary perhaps of Paranar, and an exact contemporary of the Chola ruler Karikāla and of Nannan, 'the Woman killer'. He is regarded as a separate person from the Tirumūlar of the 'Śaiva School.' This author has a number of references to the invasion of the south by the Mauryas, who, according to him, must have advanced, at least as far south as Madura and Podiyil Hill. This author, according to Nachchinārkkiniyar, the commentator, was a Brahman belonging to the family of the Sage Agastya, and belonged to the part of the country hallowed by his presence, that is the country round the Podiyil Hill in the Western Ghats in the South-West of Madura and the neighbouring parts of the Tinnevelly District of the Madras Presidency

The first reference in this author to call for notice is in Aham 15[8] where the author refers to the entry of a warlike tribe called *Kośar* into the Tuḷu Naḍu of Nannan. Aham 251 of the same author refers again to these *Kośar* and states that these people administered a crushing defeat upon their enemies near Podiyil Hill.[9] On this occasion, says the poet, Mohur not having submitted, the newly-installed 'Mauryas came up at the head of a great army,' the rolling

8 *Vide* note 3.

9 நாம்படர் கூருமருந்துயர் கேட்பி
னந்தன் வெறுக்கை யெய்தினு மற்றவட்
டங்கலர் வாழிதோழி வெல் கொடித்
துனை காலன்னபுனை தேர்க் கோசர்
தொன்மூதாலத் தரும்பிணைப் பொதியி
லின்னிசை முரசங்கடிப் பிடித்திரங்கத்
தெம்முனை சிதைத்த ஞான்றை மோகூர்ப்
பணியாமையிற் பகைதலைவந்த
மாகெழுதானை வம்ப மோரியர்
புனைதேர் நேமியுருளிய குறைத்த
விலங்கு வெள்ளருவி யறைவாயும்பர்

Aham 251. Māmūlanār.

(Mahamahopadhyaya Pandit Swaminatha Iyer's text obligingly copied by him.)

Madura. (2) The advance party of the invasion was composed of a warlike people called Kośar in one case and Vaḍukar in another. (3) The point of time to which these invasions are referrable.

In regard to point 1, the texts of this author are quite clear and unmistakeable. He is supported in regard to this statement by two others. One of them is called Paranar according to one manuscript, but the manuscript in the Madras Government Oriental Manuscripts Library of Aham 69[12] shews the author's name as Param Koṟṟanār. The language of the reference is equally clear, and quite similar in regard to the cutting of the way through a hill for the car to pass. Poem 175[13] of Puram

12 விண்பொரு நெடு (ங்) ங்குடையியறேர் மோரியர்
பொன் புனை திகிரி திரிதரக் (க்) குறைத்த
அறையிறந் தகன்றனராயினு மெனையதூஉ
நீட (ட) லர்வாழி தோழி.

Aham 69. Paramkoṟṟanār.

13 விண்பொரு நெடுவிங்குடையியறே ரோரியர்*
திண்கதிர்த் திகிரி திரிதரக் குறைத்த
வுலகவிடை கழியறைவாய் நிலைஇய
மலர்வாய் மண்டிலத்தன்ன.

Puram 175. Kaḷḷil Āttirayanār.

* Another reading :—மோரியர்.

by Kaḷḷil Attiraiyanār, celebrating the patron Adan Ungan has an equally clear reference to the army of the Mauryas cutting their way through rock to let the road go through the middle of the world. The commentator obviously was not able to understand the reference, and adopted in consequence a reading Oriyar for Moriyar, making the passage seem legendary. The far-fetched character of his comment is unmistakeable evidence of misreading. The manner of reference in all passages under consideration, makes it clear that this 'cutting' (whether a tunnel or no) was at a great distance from the Tamil country. The reference in the majority of the passages is to a lover who had gone away from his sweetheart, and this cutting is brought in much in the manner of Shakespeare's 'her husband is to Aleppo gone.' All the references are in the past tense and give evidence of the event having been of recent historical occurrence.

In respect of the Kośar and the Vadukar we have other confirmatory evidence. One passage[14] in Paraṇar, a contemporary poet with Mamulanar, states that this warlike tribe entered Nannan's territory after a battle in which Nannan lost his state elephant. This Nannan's territory is, according to certain poems, the Tuḷu-country (*Vide* Aham 15) and according to others (Narrınaı 391), Konkanam (Tamil for Konkanam, or Anglo-Indian, Konkan). That this territory actually took in parts of Konkan and Canara or Tuḷu is borne out by the fact that one of his famous hills Eḻilmalai[15] exists to-day as Saptaśaila or Ēḻilmalai about 16 miles north of Cannanore. The Kośar then entered Nannan's territory through Konkaṉ, and had a south-east trend in their movement through Kongu, (Aham 195 and Siliappadhikaram, Kongiḷan-gośar) till they reached the Podiyil Hill much farther south. These Tamil works refer to these Kośar in association with the Mauryas, almost as constituting the advanced guard of

[14] Kurumtogai 73. See note 4.

[15] Naṟṟinai 391. See Note 3. Mont D'Ely of the medieval writers. Yule's Marco. Polo. Bk. III. Ch. 24. note 1.

their army of invasion. The Rāmāyaṇa contains a reference to a people, called Kōśakāra, the equivalent of the Tamil Kośar, in the following passage :—

> ब्रह्ममालान् विदेहांश्च माळ्वान् काशि कोसलाम् ।
> मगधांश्च महाग्रामान् पुन्ड्रान् वङ्गांस्तथैवच ॥
> पत्तणं कोशकाराणां भूमिश्च रजताकरान् ।
>
> (IV. 40. 121 &c. Kumbakonam Edn.)

The city of the Kosakara finds mention among the states towards the east to which Sugrīva directed one section of his great search party. The commentary explains the centre of reference to have been the 'Sarāvati,' a river in Rajaputana which flows in a circle and loses itself in the sands. If it is permissible to locate this on the basis of the data available to us in this, the habitat of the Kōśakāra will correspond to Assam. The term Kōśakāra is explained by the commentary called Tilaka, as a people engaged in the work of rearing silk-worms and manufacturing silk. If this interpretation is correct, then there must have been in East Bengal a warlike people whose usual peaceful avocation was silk manufacture and who might have formed part of the Mauryan army. It seems to be these people who had laid hold of the hill fort Pāḷi of Nannam from which these were dislodged by the Chola king, Neydalamkanal Iḷanjētchenni, identical in all probability with the father of Karikāla, the great Chola. In this connection these people are referred to as Vaḍa Vaḍukar (the Northern Northerners) in Puram 378,[16] and Vamba Vadukar (the new Northerners) in Aham 375.[17] It is again the same general movement of the northerners that is reflected

16 தென்பரதவர் மிடல் சாய
வடவடுகர் வாளோட்டிய
நற்றார்க் கள்ளின் சோழன் கோயில்.

Puram 378. Ūnpodi Paśungudayār in honour of Ilanjētchenni destroyer of Pāḷi or Śeruppāḷi,

17 சோழர் பெருமகன்
விளங்குபுகழ் நிறுத்தவிளம் பெருஞ்சென்னி
குடிக் கடனாகலின் குறைவினைமுடிமார்
செம்புறழ் புரிசைப பாழி நூறி
வம்பவடுகர் பைந்தலைச வட்டி.

Aham 375/74 by Iḍayan Śēudan Koṟṟanār.

in Narrinai 170,[18] where the Malayamān chief of Muḷḷūr is said to have sallied out and defeated single-handed the 'Aryas' that had laid seige to the fort. We have already referred to Pulikat as the limit of Aryan land in Kuruntogai II,[19] and to the change of language when one passed either this or the hill Venkata (Tirupati).[20] These taken together seem to warrant the inference that there was a series of Aryan invasions under the Mauryas and their successors the Andhras, as distinct from Aryan settlements previous to these, and that the Tamil kings and chiefs stemmed the tide of invasion successfully so far as to rank among the allies of the great Mauryan Emperor Asoka on terms of equality, as in fact they are referred to have been in the Asoka edicts. In this connection it deserves to be noted that the same poet

18 எழுமினெழுமினெங் கொழுநற்காக்க
ஆரியர் துவன்றிய பேரிசை முள்ளூர்ப்
பலருடன் கழித்த வொள்வாள் மலையன
தொருவேற் கோடியாங்கு.

Naṟṟiṇai 170, author not known.

19 See note (1)

20 Aham 15 & Naṟṟiṇai 391. See note 3.

Mamulanar refers, in Aham 115, [21] to a chieftain Erumai of Kuḍanāḍu (parts of Mysore and Coorg). The chief's name seems to have stuck on to the country so far as to make it referrable in Tamil literature as the territory of Erumaiyūrān. Hence Asoka's Mahishamanḍala which is a good translation of Erumaināḍu might still refer to this frontier state, notwithstanding Dr. Fleet's satisfactory indentification of Māhishmati with Māndhāta on the Narmada. Māhishmati was a city—the city of Kārtavīrya-Arjuna—but there is good authority for equating the name with that of the people Mahishakas and giving it the meaning that is usually given. The connection with modern Mysore town or state, is not quite proved though it is possible to understand that the whole country or any part thereof might have been known Mahishamandala. This is only by the way now.

What is relevant to the question is that the references to the Vadukar and Aryar in

21 நண்பூவெருமை குடநாட்டன்ன.

Aham 15/14 Māmūlanār.

this latter batch are to either contemporaneous or to almost contemporaneous events. The defeat of the Aryar by the Malayamān on the one side, and the destruction of Pāḻi and the crushing of the Vamba Vadukar (newly established northerners) there by Ilanjetchenni cannot refer to the same early period as the Maurya invasions of Māmular. These have an organic connection with the defeat of the Aryas by Imayavaramban Perumśēral Ādan,[22] Pāndyan Aryappadai Kadanda Nedum Śeḻiyan [23]

22 ஆரியர் துவன்றிய பேரிசை யிமயம்
தென்னங்குமரி யொடாயிடை
மன்மீக் கூறுநர்

அமைவரலருவி யிமையம் விற்பொறித்
திமிழ் கடல்வேலித் தமிழகம் விளங்கத்
தன்கோனிறீ இத்தகைசால் சிறப்பொடு
பேரிசைமரபினாரியர் வணக்கி.

Padirruppattu I (i) 23—25 & II. பதிகம்

23 வடவாரியர்படை கடந்து
தென்றமிழ் நாடொருங்கு காணப்
புறைதீர் கற்பிற் றேவிதன்னுட
னரசுகட்டி விற்றுஞ்சிய பாண்டிய
னெடுஞ்செழியன்

Śilappadikāram XXIII, 11. 14-15.

and Karikala[24] who all lay claim to victory over the Aryas, and to having erected their respective emblems the bow, the fish and the tiger 'on the face of the Himalayas.'[25] All these seem to refer to action taken by the Tamils in concert, when the Central power in the North began to weaken, to beat back the Northerners from the South, there being perhaps in it also the Southern Hindu hostility to the Northern Buddhism. Taken together the references seem to warrant the inferences (1) that the Mauryas carried their invasions to the farthest south of India; (2) that they were in hostile occupation of forts in the northern borders of the Tamil land extending

24 இமைய வருறையுஞ் சிமையப் பிடர்த்தலைக்
கொடுவரியேற்றிக் கொள்கையிற் பெயர்வோற்கு
மாநீர்வேலி வச்சிரந ன்னாட்டுக்
கோனிறை கொடுத்த கொற்றப் பந்தரும்
மகத நன்னாட்டு வாள்வாய் வேந்தன்
பகைப்புறத்துக் கொடுத்த பட்டி மண்டபமும்
அவந்தி வேந்த னுவந்தனன் கொடுத்த.
நிவந்தோங்கு மரபிற்றோ ரணவாயிலும்.

Ibid. V. L. 98 & Commentary thereon.

25 கயலெழுதிய விமய நெற்றியி
னயலெழுதிய புலியும் வில்லும்

Opus, cit. XVII. 11, 1 & 2.

from Pulikat in the east to almost Goa in the west; and (3) that these Aryans were beaten back when the Mauryas and their successors at headquarters become too feeble or too much occupied to be able to retain their hold on the distant south.

Coming down to point 3 regarding the time of these invasions our sources do not give us any direct lead. The references to the Maurya invasions are all of them in the past and do not warrant inferences of contemporaneity, though the character of these references is unmistakeably historical. We are almost able to see the line of advance through Tuḷu into Kongu. Therefrom there is a double line, one south-eastwards through Tirukkovilur, to the Chola country perhaps as a further objective, though we have no evidence of its having gone so far; and the other through the famous historical route through the Palnis (Tam Podini) into the Pāṇḍya country up to the Podiyil Hill. These invasions must have taken place in the heyday of the Mauryan power after Chandragupta had entered into the definitive treaty with Seleucus I of Asia

(Nicator). It may be that he himself effected the conquest, or his son[26] as his father's viceroy, at Vidiśa. The invasion must have come through the later Burhanpur Road, the ancient Dakshiṇāpatha, leading from Avanti through Vidarbha into the Dekhan, and must have gone along the Western Ghats into the Tamil country avoiding Danḍāraṇyam as the Tamils called it (Sans. Danḍakāraṇyam.) The inference is supported by (1) the Tamils regarding the country north of Pulikat as having been foreign in language, (2) their regarding the locality as a border land in which cattle forays could be committed with impunity, (3) their regarding Dandāranyam as having been includ-

26 The surname Amitrachates (Gr. for Amitraghāta) for Bindusāra indicates that he was a great conqueror, as the Greeks knew him by this surname rather than by his name. The point of Dr. Fleet's objection in regard to the word Amitraghāta not being a name is not clear. It could not have been a name. In the Ramāyaṇa Kumbhakarṇa is described as Amitraghātin (VI. 60. 97 Kumbh. Edition.) We have no precedents for Gangaikonḍa, Akālavarsha, Āhavamalla &c., nor for Ajātaśatru. (J.R.A.S. 1909 p. 24 & p. 427.)

ed in the Aryan land as in the Padirruppattu[27] and in the Periplus of the Erythræan Sea[28].

The Maurya invasion and the attempt at occupation of the Tamil country should be referred to the period intervening the treaty between Seleucus and Chandragupta, and the thirteenth year of Asoka. Their dislodgment from the south must be referred to the period

27 ஈன்றமகன்
றண்டாரணியத்துக் கோட்பட்டவருடையைத்
தொண்டியுட்டந்து கொடுப்பித்துப் பார்ப்பார்க்கு.

Commentary.

இதன் பதிகத்துத் தண்டாரணிய மென்றது ஆரிய நாட்டில் உள்ளதோர் நாடு.

Padirrupattu, VI. பதிகம்.

28 Beyond Barygaza the adjoining coast extends in a straight line from north to south; and so this region is called Dachinabades, for *dachanos* in the language of the natives means "south". The inland country back from the coast toward the east comprises many desert regions and great mountains; and all kinds of wild beasts—leopards, elephants, enormous serpents, hyenas, and baboons of many sorts; and many populous nations, as far as the Ganges.

W. Schoff's Edn. p. 43.

of internal weakness and foreign invasions between the fall of the Sungas and the rise of the Āndhrabhṛtyas of the Purāṇas which period various lines of evidence indicate as being capable of inclusion in the period of Mamulanar and others of the third Tamil Academy of Madura.

CHAPTER III.

THE DAWN OF THE CHRISTIAN ERA

I. South Indian Commerce

INDIA the wonderland of the east, as it is even now called, was made known to the west, as it never was before, when the world conqueror, Alexander the Great, forced open her gates on the north-west. Our knowledge of India at all of a definite character may be said to extend no farther than this period, as, according to the most recent authority, his connection with India was not much more than a great raid. It is matter of common knowledge that he had to give up his idea of carrying his conquests right up to the eastern limits of the land, (according to his own notion of the configuration of the earth), owing to a mutiny among his soldiers headed by his cavalry commander Koinos. Before leaving India, however, he divided his conquests on this side of the Indian Caucasus into three viceroyalties as follows:

I. Paropanisadae, the country west of the Indus, with Oxyartes, the father of Roxana, for its viceroy.

II. The Punjab including in it the kingdom of Taxila, and that of Porus; that of the Sophytes together with the territories of the Oxydrachoi and the Malloi, under the Viceroy Philip, son of Machetas; leaving the civil administration in the hands of the native princes.

III. Sindh including the kingdom of Mousikanos, Oxykanos, Sambus and Maeris of Patalene under Peithon, the son of Agenor, for its viceroy.

Philip was murdered in a mutiny, before the death of Alexander, and his place was taken by Eudamos who remained in India till called away in 317 B.C. to help Eumenes against Antigonus of Asia, the most powerful among the Diadochi. When the Macedonian Empire was partitioned a second time in 321 B.C. (consequent on the death of Perdiccas, the regent of the first partition,) the Indian province, east of the Indus, was left out of account, as Peithon had to withdraw to the western bank of the great river. About 305 B. C. Seleucus Nikator made an attempt to revive the empire of Alexander in this region, but had to relinquish his hold upon the whole of Afghanistan, and enter into a humiliating treaty with Chandragupta, the Maurya emperor of India. This personage is believed to have been in the camp of Alexander in the Punjab, and, thrown upon his own resources as the great Macedonian turned away from the banks of the Ravi, he took advantage of the confusion resulting from the departure of Alexander to overthrow the Greek provinces in India, and the ruling Nanda in Magadha, before he set himself up as the first Emperor of India, hitherto known to history. In the course of fifteen years he was able to make himself so strong as to fight Seleucus, not only on equal terms but also to extort from him such a valuable cession of territory as Afghanistan up to the Hindu-Kush. For three generations this dynasty held its power undiminished. His grandson Asoka, the great Buddhist Emperor of India, was able to hold his own with the successors of Seleucus, and maintained with them the diplomatic relations thus begun by his grandfather. It seems to be well attested that both Seleucus Nikator and Ptolemy Philadelphus had sent ambassadors to the courts of Chandragupta and Bindusāra, although scholars are not wanting yet who consider the particular edict of Asoka a mere boast. With the death of Asoka about 230 B. C. the Mauryan empire loses its hold upon the more powerful and distant of its vassals, and the days of the dynasty are numbered.

From this event to the year A.D. 319 the date of the rise to power of the Imperial Guptas, the history of India is yet quite uncertain, although we are able to gain a few glimpses as to the general features of the history of that period. The Asiatic empire of the Seleucidae was attacked simultaneously by the Romans and the Gauls from the west and north-west, and the Parthians from the east. About the beginning of the second century B. C., Parthia made good her independence under Arsakes Mithridates I, and Baktria under Eukratides.[1] This was but the reflex action of the movements of the nomad tribes in the far-off plains of Mongolia. The great tribe of the Hiung-nu fell with all the hostility of immediate neighbours upon the Yueh-chi, and dislodged them from their then habitat in the plains of Zungaria. These in their turn fell upon the Wu-sung, killed the Wu-sung chieftain in battle, and marched further upon the region then in the occupation of the Se, Sok or Sakas. These last had to make room for them along the right bank of the Oxus and occupy the country protected by the Indian Caucasus. The Yueh-chi were themselves defeated by the son of the late Wu-sung chieftain. When his father fell in battle he found a secure asylum with the Hiung-nu, who now helped him to regain his lost patrimony. It was in the course of these movements that the Śakas and possibly some of the Hiung-nu moved down the Kabul valley into India, and occupied the country on the right bank of the Indus, another

[1] V. A. Smith, Early History of India, p. 210 ff.

body probably from the region of Seistan occupying right down even to Gujarat. It is one of their out-settlements on the Jumna that the coins and other antiquities of Muttra would seem to warrant.

While all this was taking place across the borders of India, in India itself there was going forward a revolution of no less consequence. The Mauryan empire was overthrown by Pushyamitra Sunga, the Maurya general, in spite of the loyalist minister, a brother-in-law of Yegnasena Śātakarṇi of the Dekhan. The usurper's strength was tried by a triple war:—(1) against Menander, ruler of Kabul; (2) against Kharavēla, the Kalinga ruler of Orissa; (3) against the loyalist Yegnasēna and in behalf of a counter-claimant to the throne of the kingdom of Vidharba. Though for the time successful against all these, the empire had suffered vital injuries. The Dekhan kingdom or viceroyalty becomes so powerful that the Andhras establish an imperial position themselves, and render their quota of service by holding out against the Śaka invaders from the north-west and west. It must have been in the course of these wars that the occasion should have arisen for the founding of the era which now goes by the name of Vikramāditya and that under the name of Śaka. As to both these eras and the circumstances of their origin, there is very considerable difference of opinion among scholars. In the course of the political shiftings described above, a clan of the Yueh-chi, by name Kushāna, was able to push its way into India, and establish a kingdom in the Punjab including Kashmir. The greatest ruler among them, whose empire came into touch with the Chinese Empire on the one side and the Parthian on the other, is Kanishka, the Constantine of the Buddhism of the greater vehicle (Mahayana Buddhism). Learned scholars associate him with both the eras above referred to, while there are yet others, who would dissociate him from either and refer him to a period later than both. None of them, however, take him beyond the period I have marked at the beginning. At the very beginning of the Christian era then the Punjab and the frontier province, including Kashmir, were under the Kushānas or their immediate predecessors or their successors. Gujarat and Malva, including northern Konkan, were under the Sakas.

During the period marked out above, we have been passing from the supremacy of Buddhism (if such an expression can be regarded as appropriate at all), through a reassertion of the Brahman ascendancy, on to a final compromise, ending on the one side in Mahāyānist Buddhism, and on the other, in the Hinduism of the Gita. For as Professor Kern maintains, on the authority of the Tibetan historian Taranatha and the Saddharma-puṇḍarīka, the founder of the Mādhyamika school of Buddhism, Nagarjuna, was a disciple of the Brahman Rāhuḷabhadra who was much indebted to Sage Krishna. Paraphrased, this means no less than that these teachers drew a part of their inspiration from the Gita.[2] This is borne out by the importance that attaches to Bhakti (devotion) in Mahayanist Buddhism and later Hinduism.

During all this period of active mutations

[2] Manual of Indian Buddhism, p. 122.

both in religion and politics, South India would appear to have been out of this great vortex. This is a delusion due more to lack of information than to a lack of history. The edicts of Asoka, as was stated already, mention the Chola, Pāṇḍya, Kērala, Satiyaputra and Ceylon among those with whom he entered into diplomatic relations. He thought it worth his while to send his son and daughter to Ceylon as missionaries. These facts put it beyond a doubt that there was some communication between Magadha and Ceylon, generally by way of the sea. It is now clear from Chapter II that the neighbouring coast was also brought into touch with the north, by way of land. The Ceylonese tradition, as embodied in the *Mahāvaṁśa*, is quite in support of this conclusion. Between the Mahārāshṭra and Malva there was a great trunk road notwithstanding the great forest region between them. This road it is that has given us the name Dekhan (Dakshiṇāpathā). Most likely this road wound its way over the hills by way of Burhanpur into western Malva. The middle region was the forest, which it continued to be even up to the days of Harsha.

During this period, and for a long time after, Hindustan (the country north of the Vindhyas) kept touch with the outer world by way of land mainly ; the south kept itself in contact with the rest of the world chiefly by way of the sea. That the Hindus did not always wait for others to come to them for goods is in evidence in a variety of ways. There is first the statement of Cornelius Nepos, who says that Q.Metellus Celer received from the king of the Suevi some Indians, who had been driven by storm into Germany in the course of a voyage of commerce. [3] This is quite a precise fact, and is borne out by a number of tales of voyages with the horrors attending navigation depicted in the liveliest colours in certain classes of writings both in Sanskrit and Tamil. Among the places mentioned in the latter classes of sources are those in the East Indian Archipelago, such as Java(Śāvham), Sambhava (Karpūrasambhavam), Katāha (Sumatra), and

3 1 Macrindle, Ancient India. p. 110.

Kālahm (Burma) not to mention China. It may now be taken for certain that in the sixth and fifth centuries B.C. there was considerable intercourse with Babylonia [4] and through her with Assyria and the further West. The Bavēru Jātaka is certain proof of this intercourse by way of the sea. It would thus appear that there was some very considerable activity in maritime commerce. They used to have lighthouses to warn ships and one such is described at the great port at the mouth of the Kavery, a brick tower or a big palmyra trunk carrying on the top of it a huge oil lamp.

The classical geographers, the author of the Periplus and Ptolemy the geographer, that date respectively about A. D. 80 and A.D. 150, exhibit knowledge of a division of the country almost the same as the three divisions indicated in chapter I. The author of The Periplus [5] begins his account of the

4 The Early Commerce of Babylon with India : 700—300 B.C. by J. Kennedy J.R.A.S. 1898, pp. 241—288.

5 The Periplus of the Erythræan Sea translated and edited by W. H. Schoff. Secs. 42 to 66.

west of India with the Indus (Sinthus). He says that the river had seven mouths, shallow and marshy, and therefore not navigable. On the shore of the central channel was the seaport Barbaricum with a capital in the interior of the Scythians called Minnagara. (The city of the Min, Scythians); the port Barbaricum has not generally been identified. It seems to be the Sanskrit Barbaraka (belonging to the country of the Barbara, and therefore the port of the people, Barbara, perhaps the same as the Gk. barbarian). Passing down from there, the Periplus comes down the Surāshsṭra coast (Syrashtrene) and the Rann of Couch (Eirinon) sailing across what is the Gulf of Kambay, he takes us to Barygaza (Sans. Barukacha, Mod. Broach). With this is supposed to begin Ariaca "which is the beginning of the kingdom of Nambanus and *of all India.*" This division of that part of the country into Ariaca is also made by Ptolemy, and in the ports given along this portion of Ariaca both Ptolemy and the Periplus agree except for the omission of some in the latter. The southern limit of this coast is Tindis according to both. The corresponding portion of the country inland is described in the Periplus as Ābhira, the coast portion being Surāshṭra, as was already stated. This part of the country is described as a fertile country producing wheat, rice, sesame oil and clarified butter; cotton and coarser sorts of cloth made therefrom; pasturing of cattle seems an important occupation and the people are described as of great stature and dark in colour. The chief point to note here in connection with this statement of the Periplus is that the coast under reference is described as the beginning of the kingdom of Nambanus and of all India. The latter expression indicates clearly that whoever Nambanus was, he was at the time that the Periplus was written known to the outside world as the king of India. In other-words, it seems to have been the days of the Andhra empire of Magadha. The name Nambanus itself is a correction of the text which has Mambarus, and Mambarus might well be the Lambodara of the pauranic list of the Sātavāhanas or the Andhras of the Dekhan. The chronology of the early rulers of these Sātavāhanas cannot yet be regarded as being definitely settled and at any rate the expression in the text seems of very doubtful application to identify Nambanus with Nahapana, the Kshaharatta ruler. After describing the difficulties of navigating up to the port of Broach and the arrangement made by the ruler for piloting the vessels safely into the port, the Periplus proceeds to give the countries inland set over against that coast between Barbaricum at the mouth of the Indus obviously and Broach. He gives among them Araṭṭas of the Punjab, the Arachosii of Southern Afghanistan, the Gandaraei (Sanskrit, Gāndhāra) and the people of Poclais (Sans. Pushkalāvati) both in the region between the Kabul and the Indus in Northern Afghanistan including also the Northern portions of the Punjab, where was also the city of Alexandria. Bucephalus located very near the Jhelum. Beyond these he says were the warlike Bactrians. He gives an interesting fact that in his day coins bearing Greek inscriptions or Greek legends were prevalent in the country round Broach, and they contained, according to the Periplus, the devices of the

Greek Rulers succeeding Alexander among them Apollodotus and Menander. Coming further East from these countries he speaks of Ozene (Ujjain), and refers to it as the former royal capital. Passing over all that he says about the trade of Broach which is not to our present purpose, we come in Sec. 50 to another statement which is of interest to us He says " beyond Barigasa the adjoining coast extends in a straight line from north to south and so this region is called Dachinabades, for Dachan in the language of the natives means "south." The inland country back from the coast towards the east comprises many desert regions and great mountains; and all kinds of wild beasts, leopards, tigers, elephants, enormous serpents, hyenas, and baboons of many sorts, and many populous nations as far as the Ganges." This clearly indicates that he describes the whole of the region known as the Dakšhināpatha or the Deccan, and the Daṇḍakāraṇyam of the Sanskrit writers; the central region of India corresponding to our modern division of the Dekhan. He then describes the interior marts of Paitan and

Tagara, and of the sea-ports along the coast till he reached Naura and Tindis, the first marts of Damirica as he calls them (Sanskrit Dramiḍaca, the correct equivalent of the Greek). Damirica, sometimes written by error Lymirica, is the Sanskrit Dramiḍaca which the author must have heard in contradistinction to *Ariaca*. It is perhaps a little far-fetched to see in it Tamiḻakam. With Tindis began according to both Ptolemy and the Periplus, the kingdom of Cherabothra (Cheraputra or Keralaputra). The next port of importance we come to, is 50 miles from Tindis again at the mouth of a river; the port called Muziris (Muyiri or Muŝiri of the Tamils, the modern Cranganore). Fifty miles further south was the sea-port of Nelcynda which the late Mr. Kanakasabhai Pillai correctly identified with Nirkunṛam in the country of the Pāṇḍyas. This place was situated about ten or twelve miles in the interior with an out-port at the mouth of the river, the village Bacara-Vaikkarai, as we know it now. The kings of both these market towns, the Periplus says "live in the interior." The imports into Muziris are given "as a great quantity of coin; topaz, thin clothing, not much; figured linens, antimony, coral, crude glass, copper, tin, lead; wine not much but as much as at Barigaza; realgar and orpiment; and wheat only for the sailors, for this is not dealt in by the merchants there." The exports from this place are the "pepper coming from 'Kottanora (Kuṭṭu Nāḍu in the interior) "great quantities of fine pearls" ivory, silk cloth, spikenard from the Ganges, Malabathrum from the interior, transparent stones of all kinds, diamonds and saphires and tortoise-shell. "That from the Chryse island (golden) and that taken from among the islands along the coast of Damirica." One may so far compare this statement with the following two extracts from Tamil Literature:—

6 கலந்தந்த பொற்பரிசம்
கழித்தோணியார்க் கரை சேர்க்குந்து
மலைத்தாரமுங் கடற்றாரமுந்
தலைப்பெய்துவருநர்க்கீயும்
புனலங்கள்ளின் பொலந்தார்க்குட்டுவன்
முழங்குகடல் முழவின் முசிறியன்ன.

பரணர். Puram 343.

Beyond Vaikkarai, the Periplus refers to the dark-red mountains and of the district (stretching along the coast towards the south "Paralia" generally taken as equivalent to Pural, coast) ; the first port in this coast region is what he calls Balita, identified with Varkkali or Janārdhanam, which in those days had a fine harbour and a village by the sea-shore. Then comes Kumāri with a cape and a harbour. It is also referred to as a holy bathing place, and the coast region is then described as extending eastwards till it reaches Korkai " where the pearl fisheries are," and the Periplus offers the interesting piece of information, " that they are worked by condemned criminals." Then follows another coast region with a region inland called according to the Periplus Argaru, taken to be the equivalent of Uraiyur. These two regions of the coast country are somewhat differently named in Ptolemy. He called the region

சேரலர்சுள் ளியம்பேரியாற்று வெண்ணுரைகலங்க
யவனர்தந் தவினைமாணன் கலம்
பொன்னொடு வந்து கறியொடு பெயரும்
வளங்கெழுமு சிறியரர்ப்பெழ,
காட்டூர்த்தாயங்கண்ணன். Aham 148.

between Nirkuṉṟum and Camorin as in the country of Aioi. (Tamil Āay). Then follows the region which he calls Kareoi (Tamil Karai or Karaiyar, a class of fisherfolk) and the coast country extending from Korkai upwards is spoken of by Ptolemy in two divisions. The country of the Batoi (Tamil Vettuvar) and Porālia in the country of the Toringoi (error for Soringoi, Cholas). The exports from this region according to the Periplus are: the pearls [7] gathered from part of what is brought at any time from

[7] Pliny says: (Chap. IX 54—58.)

"Our ladies glory in having pearls suspended from their fingers, or two or three of them dangling from their ears, delighted even with the rattling of the pearls as they knock against each other; and now, at the present day, the poorer classes are even affecting them, as people are in the habit of saying, that 'a pearl worn by a woman in public is as good as a lictor walking before her.' Nay, even more than this, they put them on their feet, and that, not only on the laces of their sandals but all over the shoes; it is not enough to wear pearls, but they must tread upon them, and walk with them under foot as well.

"I once saw Lollia Paulina, the wife of the Emperor Caius—it was not at any public festival, or any solemn ceremonial, but only at an ordinary betrothal entertain-

there and a kind of fine muslin called Argaratic. The most important ports mentioned in this region by the Periplus are three: Camara (identified with Kaveripatnam), Poduca (may be a Puduvai) and it is doubtful whether it stands for Pondicherry or a place in the vicinity. Then Sopatma (Tamil Śopaṭṭaṇam or fortified port). There come ships from what he calls Damirica and from the north for the exchange of commodities. Here the Periplus has an important statement to

ment—covered with emeralds and pearls, which shone in alternate layers upon her head, in her hair, in her wreaths, in her ears, upon her neck, in her bracelets, and on her fingers, and the value of which amounted in all to 40,000,000 sesterces; indeed she was prepared at once to prove the fact, by showing the receipts and acquittances. Nor were these any presents made by a prodigal potentate, but treasures which had descended to her from her grandfather, and obtained by the spoliation of the provinces. Such are the fruits of plunder and extortion! It was for this reason that M. Lollius was held so infamous all over the East for the presents which he extorted from the kings; the result of which was, that he was denied the friendship of Caius Cæsar, and took poison; and all this was done, I say, that his granddaughter might be seen, by the glare of lamps, covered all over with jewels to the amount of forty millions of sesterces!"

make in respect of the capacity for navigation of the Tamiis. In these ports that he mentions, he says were ships of two kinds, those intended for coasting voyages as far as Damirica, as he calls it; these were small and large and are called by him Sangara. Those intended however, for the voyages to Chryse and to the Ganges were called, according to him, Colandia, and are described as very large. The term Chryse which in Greek is the equivalent of gold, seems to refer to Suvarnnabhumi in Sanskrit, and has been identified with the Malaya Peninsula, spoken of by the Periplus in another place as an island. That it indicates the region about the Malaya Peninsula is clear from what he says in regard to the direction of the land; "just opposite this river (Ganges) there is an island in the ocean the last port of the inhabited world to the east under the rising sun itself; it is called Chryse and it has the best tortoise-shell of all the places on the Erythræan Sea. There are said to be imported into these ports everything that is made in Damirica "the greatest part of what is got from

Egypt." Then he proceeds to mention Palæsimundu, "called by the ancients Taprobane." Further north from this, according to him, was the region Masalia and further north of this Dosarene (Sans. Daśārṇa). Ptolemy however interpolates between the Chola coast and Maisalia (Masalia of the Periplus) the country of the Arouvarnoi or Arvarnoi (the Aruvalar of the Tamils) whose country was known to the Tamils in two divisions Aruvānāḍu and Aruvā Vada Talai (northern Aruva) which would take us more or less close to the mouth of the Krishna river, the Maisalos of Ptolemy.

Of the trade of this coast, the most important ports are the three referred to already, and the imports of trade are set down "Everything made in Damirica and the greatest part of what is brought at any time from Egypt comes here together with most kinds of all the things that are brought from Damirica and of those that are carried through Paralia."

We have similar reference to the imports at Kaveripatam in the Tamil work Paṭṭinappāli "horses were brought from distant lands beyond the seas, pepper was brought in ships, gold and precious stones came from the northern mountains, sandal and akhir came from the mountains towards the west, pearls from the southern seas and coral from the eastern seas. The produce of the regions watered by the Ganges; all that is grown on the banks of the Kavery; articles of food from Īḻam or Ceylon and the manufactures of Kāḻakam in Burma."[8] This looks like a re-statement in a somewhat expanded form of what is found briefly stated in the Periplus. Such was the condition of industry and commerce of this land as far as it is possible for us to picture this condition from the evidence available to us.

II. *Internal condition: political, industrial &c.*

To take up the political geography of south India as a whole then, the country south of the Krishna was divided among 'the three crowned kings' and seven chieftains, with an eighth coming somewhat later. There were

8 Paṭṭinappālai ll. 127 ff. and Mr. Kanakasabhai's Tamils 1,800 years ago, p. 27.

a host of minor chieftains of lesser repute. It is the coast region and the more open country that belonged to the kings, while the middle regions of hills and forests belonged to the chieftains, and perhaps even a few tribes (Nagas and others). The east coast from near the mouth of the Krishna to the south of Tondi in the Zamindari of Ramnad, belonged to the Chola, although midway between the kingdom proper and its northern viceroyalty of Kanchi lay the hill-country round Tirukoilur, in the possession of a class of chieftains named Malayaman, very often loyal supporters of their suzerain, occasionally truculent and rebellious. South of the Chola kingdom lay that of the Pāṇḍya, which extended from coast to coast, and embraced within its borders the modern districts of Madura and Tinnevelli, and the State of Travancore, taking in also a part of Coimbatore and Cochin. This included in it the chieftaincies of Āay (the Aioi of Ptolemy) round the Podyil hill in the western ghats, and of Evvi round about the port of Korkai in Tinnevelli. There were besides the domains of Pēhan round the Palnis which comes under their sphere of influence as well. North of this and along the western ghats on the sea-side lay the territory of the Chera : a territory stretching right across the Palghat gap through Salem and Coimbatore. South Mysore was parcelled out among a number of chieftains corresponding to the modern Palayagars, whose allegiance was at the disposal of either, but the more powerful, of their neighbour kings. Such were the Irungō of Arayam, Pāri of Parambunad, Adiyamān of Tagadūr (Dharmapuri) and Ori of the Kolli-malais. The first of these was within the Mysore territory proper, and to the east of his domain lay the Gangas, and Kongu to the south. The northern frontier of the Tamil land was held by Nannan of the Tuḷu country in the West, and Pulli of Vēngaḍam (Tirupati) in the east, the further north having been the land of the Aryas (Vaḍukar) and Dandā-raṇyam (Sans. Danḍakāraṇyam).

These chieftaincies were the bone of contention between the Cholas and the Cheras. When the period under treatment begins, the

Cholas are supreme under Karikala, who ascended the throne, probably after defeating the Chēra and Pāṇḍya in a battle at Veṇṇil (Koilveṇṇi as it is now called) in the Tanjore district. He was a remarkable sovereign who, in many ways, contributed to the permanent welfare of his subjects, and has consequently been handed down to posterity as a beneficent and wise monarch. He constructed the embankments for the Kavery, and his chief port Puhar was the great emporium of the east coast. His reign was long and, taken along with those of his two predecessors and the successor next following him, constitutes the period of the first Chola ascendancy in the south. In the reign of his successor a great catastrophe befell Puhar, and the city and port were both destroyed. This was a hard blow to the ascendancy of the Cholas. But Karikāla had, after defeating his contemporary Chera, given one of his daughters in marriage to the son of his vanquished rival. This alliance stood the Cholas in good stead. Karikāla's successor began his reign with a victory, which his heir-apparent won for him, against the Chera and Pāṇḍya combined, at Kāriyār, probably in the Salem district. When Puhar was destroyed there was a civil war, owing perhaps to the untimely death of the young Chola prince ; and the Chera ruler for the time being, advanced through the central region. He intervened in favour of his cousins with effect, as against the rival claimants of royal blood, and restored the Chola dynasty to some power ; but the ascendancy surely enough passed from them to the Chera. The Chera ascendancy under the Red-Chera (Śenguṭṭuvan) lasted only one generation ; in the reign of his successor the Pāṇḍyas rose to greater importance and the Chera suffered defeat and imprisonment at his hands. This Pāṇḍya ascendancy probably lasted on somewhat longer till about the rise of the Pallavas in Kanchi. This course of the political centre of gravity in southern India is borne out in very important particulars by the Ceylon Chronicle, called the *Mahāvamśa*. According to this work, the Cholas were naturally the greatest enemies of the Singalese rulers. There were usurpers from the Chola country in Ceylon in the first century B.C.; and there were invasions and counter-invasions as well. On one occasion the Chola invaders carried away 12,000 inhabitants of Ceylon and set them to work at 'the Kavery' as the Chronicle has it.[9] This looks very much like an exploit of Karikāla seeing that it was he who built the city of Puhār. King Gajabāhu of Ceylon was present at the invitation of the Red-Chera, to witness the celebration of a sacrifice and the consecration of the temple to the 'Chaste Lady' (Pattini Dēvi) at Vanji, on the west coast.

The ascendancy of the Chera, however, passed away, as already mentioned, to the Pāṇḍyas in the course of one single generation. The Red-Chera was succeeded by his son, 'the Chera of the elephant look,' who was his father's viceroy at Tondi, and figured prominently in the wars of his predecessor in the middle region. He was defeated and taken prisoner in a battle, which he had to fight with the contemporary Pāṇḍyan, designated the victor, at Talayālangānam. With this

[9] Upham's Mahāvamsa, Vol. i, p. 228.

mishap to the ruler the Chera ascendancy passes away. The Pāṇḍyans of Madura take their turn now, and continued to hold the position of hegemony up to the time that the Pallavas rise into importance. This, in brief and in very general terms, was the political history of South India at the beginning and during the early centuries of the Christian Era.

Passing on from the political to the industrial condition of India, we have already described the principal sea-ports, both on the western and eastern seaboard. If, as has been pointed out, there were so many thriving ports and, if foreign merchants sought these for trade at considerable risk of pirates and, if there was so much enterprise in sea-going among the inhabitants of the country itself, the conclusion is irresistible that the country had a prosperous industry, and so, on examination, it appears certainly, to have been. Apart from the complaints of Petronius that fashionable Roman ladies exposed their charms much too immodestly by clothing themselves in the 'webs of woven wind', as he called the muslins imported from India, Pliny says that India drained the Roman empire annually to the extent of 55,000,000 sesterces, equal to £486, 979[10] sending in return goods which sold at a hundred times their value in India.[11] He also remarks in another place, 'this is the price we pay for our luxuries and our women.'

That the industrial arts had received attention and cultivation in early times in India is in evidence to the satisfaction of the most sceptical mind. The early Tamils divided arts into six groups: ploughing (meaning thereby agriculture), handicrafts, painting, commerce and trade, the learned arts, and lastly the fine arts. Of these, agriculture and commerce were regarded as of the first importance. Flourishing trade pre-supposes a volume of industry, the principal of which was weaving then, as it also has been until recently. Cotton, silk and wool seem to have been the materials that

10 Mommhen gives the total £ 11,000,000, £ 6,000,000 for Arabia, £ 5,000,000 for India.

11 Malabar Manual. Vol. 1, pp. 150-1.

were wrought into cloths. Among the woollens we find mention of manufactures from the wool of rats, which was regarded as particularly warm. There are thirty varieties of silks mentioned, each with a distinctive appellation of its own, as distinguished from the imported silks of China which had a separate name. The character of the cotton stuffs that were manufactured is indicated by the comparisons instituted between them and, 'sloughs of serpents' or 'vapour from milk' and the general description of these as 'those fine textures the thread of which could not be followed even by the eye.'

The chief exports from the country, as the author of the Periplus says, were these: 'The produce of the soil like pepper, great quantities of the best pearl are likewise purchased here, ivory, silk in the web, spikenard from the Ganges, Malabathrum from the countries further to the east, transparent stones of all sorts, diamonds, rubies and tortoise-shell from the golden Chersonese or from the islands off the coast of Damirike. This is all from the port of Muziris on the west coast.

He goes on to say: 'There is a great resort of shipping to this port for pepper and malabathrum; the merchants bring out a large quantity of spice, and their other imports are topazes, stibium, coral, flint, glass, brass, and lead, a small quantity of wine as profitable as at Barugaza, cinnabar, fine cloth, arsenic and wheat, not for sale but for the use of the crew. That Pliny's complaint about the drain was neither imaginary nor hypersensitive is in evidence in a passage descriptive of Muziris in one of the ancient classics of Tamil literature.[12] 'Musiri to which come the well-rigged ships of the Yavanas, bringing gold and taking away spices in exchange.'

Regarding the trade of the east coast, here follows to imports into of Puhar: 'Horses were brought from distant lands beyond the seas, pepper was brought in ships: gold and precious stones came from the northern mountains towards the west; pearl from the southern seas and coral from the eastern seas. The produce of the region watered by the Ganges;

[12] See note 6 p. 120 above.

all that is grown on the banks of the Kavery; articles of food from Īlam (Ceylon) and the manufactures of Kālaham (Burma), [13] were brought there for sale as was stated already. The products of particular importance received in the port of Tondi (East or Chola Tondi in the Ramnad Dt.) are aghir (a kind of black aromatic wood), fine silk, camphor, silk stuff (from China), candy, sandal, scents; and these articles and salt were carried into the interior by means of wagons drawn by teams of oxen, slowly trudging along through town and village, effecting exchanges with commodities for export. Tolls were paid on the way, and the journey from the coast up the plateau and back again occupied many months. A brisk and thriving commerce with the corresponding volume of internal trade argues peace, and the period to which the above description will apply must have been a period of general peace in the Peninsula. They did not forget in those days to maintain a regular customs establishment, the officials of which

[13] Paṭṭinapālai, 127 ff, and The Tamils 1800 years ago p. 27.

piled up the grain and stored up the things that could not immediately be measured and appraised, leaving them in the dockyards carefully sealed with the tiger signet of the king.[14]

The Tamils built their own ships; and in the other crafts of the skilled artisan they seem to have attained some proficiency, though they availed themselves of experts from distant places. In the building of the royal palace at Puhar, skilled artisans from Magadha, mechanics from Marāḍam (Mahratta), smiths from Avanti (Malva), carpenters from Yavana, worked[15] together with the artisans of the Tamil land. There is mention of a temple of the most beautiful workmanship in the same city, built by the Gurjjaras.[16] In the building of forts and in the providing of them with weapons and missiles, both for offence and defence, the Tamils had attained to something like perfection. Twenty-four such weapons are mentioned among the defences of Madura.

14 Paṭṭinappālai, 134-6.

15 Maṇimēkhalai, Canto xix, 11˙107 and ff.

16 Ibid xviii. 1, 145.

Passing from the industrial to the literary, social and religious condition of the south, which we have so far been considering, we have again to do with the three kingdoms, each with a capital city and a premier port. The Cholas had their capital at Uraiyūr, with Puhar for an alternative capital and chief port; the Pāndyas had their capital at Madura, with the port and premier viceroyalty at Korkai; the Cheras had their capital at Vanji, with the principal port and viceroyalty at Tondi. The Cholas had their premier viceroy, who was generally the heir apparent, or at least a prince of the blood, at Kanchi. These towns and ports, therefore, bulk very largely in the literature and literary traditions of the period. The road from Kanchi to Trichinopoly appears to have passed through Tirukkoilur. From Trichinopoly (*i.e.* Uraiyūr) to Madura it lay along the more arid parts of the Tanjore district to Koḍumbai in the state of Pudukotta, and thence to Neḍuṁguḷam; from which place the road broke into three, and led up to Madura in three branches. From this last town a road kept close to the banks of the river Vaigai up to the Palnis; and from there it went up the hills and down again along the banks of the Periyār to the town of Vanji, situated near its mouth. There were also other roads besides; one at least, from Vanji to the modern Karoor and thence on to Tirukkoilūr.

These roads were not safe in all parts alike, there being certain portions of them that passed through desert regions, inhabited by wild tribes, who were a cause of terror to the wayfarers, particularly those who had something to lose, notwithstanding the fact that robbery was punished with nothing short of impalement. Journeys were none the less frequent for purposes of pilgrimage, or in search of patronage for learning, or for the profits of commerce.

The rulers in those days held before them high ideals of government. Their absolute authority was limited by the 'five great assemblies, as they were called, of ministers, priests generals, heralds, (spies), and ambassadors. These may be the same as the Pancha-mahā-pradhānas of Sanskrit, and may be the same as the Mahamatras associated with the princely viceroys of the Asoka Inscriptions. There appear to have been a general permit for a learned Brahman to speak his mind in any durbar ; and these Brahmans often gave out their opinions most fearlessly. This privilege was similarly accorded also to men of learning. I give a few instances in illustration. A Brahman pilgrim from the Chola country happened to be present at the Chera court, when the Chera King gave orders to his ministers to set his army in motion to avenge an insult that some northern princes, he was told, had given him. The minister's remonstrance and the reluctance of the general were overruled. This Brahman got up and pointed out, in a speech, that he had warred for the fifty years of his reign in order to safeguard his earthly interests but had done very little to provide for himself in the life to come. Of course the expedition was countermanded, and the king began to make provision for the future. A young Pāṇḍya king of the next generation showed himself too enthusiastic for war, and it fell to the lot of one of the poets at court to wean him of this war craze. In a poem of 850 lines he conveyed the hint to the king.[17] If language can be conceived as the art of concealing thought, here is an instance par excellence. The next instance takes us to the court of Vaiyyāvikkōnperum-Pēhan who neglected his wife Kaṇṇaki. A number of poets of the first rank interceded and restored him to her. The next case that I will mention here is that of a poet, who enjoyed the patronage of successive Chola rulers. He found that at the end of a civil war the victorious Chola was about to put to death his vanquished cousin. The poet pointed out that the victory tarnished the good name of the Cholas, quite as much as the defeat, and that he did not know whether to rejoice for the victorious Chola or weep for the vanquished one. The intercession was certainly effective. These illustrations show in addition the respect that learning commanded. I shall permit myself one more illustration to show this respect. The warlike Paṇḍya referred to already, came to the throne young. He

17 This is the famous piece known as Maduraikkanji, one of the Pattuppattu collection.

had immediately to go to war against a combination of his two neighbours and his court was naturally anxious as to the result. The young prince in a poem, full of poetic grace assured them that he would return victorious and that if he should fail, the poets of his court including Māngudi Marudan. might cease to attend.

The ideal of justice set before them in those days was something unattainable. They strove their utmost to attain to the sublimity of their ideal ; and a king was judged good or bad upon the degree of success he achieved in this particular branch of his duties. 'Oh the king he is to blame if the rains fail ; he is to blame if woman go astray. What is there in a king's estate, except perpetual anxiety, that people should envy the position of a king for!' Learning went in search of patronage. There must have been a very considerable output of literature. It was doubtless to check the growth of the weed of learning that a body of censors called the Śangam must have been instituted. It is a number of works, which are believed to have received the imprimatur of this learned body, that has been the source of all this information regarding this period. This is not the place to enter into the question of the origin of Tamil literature; or of its independence or otherwise; or of its connexion with the literature of Sanskrit. But I may remark in passing that Tamil literature (as distinct from language) cannot lay claim to that independence that its votaries demand for it with more zeal than argument. Learning was somewhat widespread and much sought after. Women had their share of learning, as the number of women poets indicates. Nor was this learning confined to the Brahman although he was the sole custodian of the northern lore.'

In matters religious there was a happy confusion. Jains, Buddhists, Brahmans, Śaivas, Vaishṇavas, and people of other persuasions both major and minor, all lived together and at peace with one another. 'There were splendid temples in the city dedicated to the worship of the celestial tree Kalpaka, (the wish giving tree), the celestial elephant Airāvata, Vajrāyuda (the thunderbolt of Indra), Baladeva,

Sūrya, Chandra, Śiva, Subramaṇya, Sātavāhana, (Aiyanār in Tamil or Sāsta in Mal. and Sans :) Jina or Nirgratha, Kama (god of love), and Yama (God of death). There were seven vihāras reputed to have been built by Indra, the king of the gods, in which dwelt no less than 300 monks (Buddhistic). The temple of Yama was outstide the walls of the town, in the burial ground in the city of Puhar, the capital of the Cholas. The three rival systems of the Brahmans, and those of the Jains and Buddhists flourished together each with its own clientele unhampered by the others in the prosecution of its own holy rights. The Brahman was not regarded an inconvenience, but the general feeling was that he was indispensable to the prosperity of the state. A devout Buddhist and an ascetic Jain prince both speak of him with great respect. He was the custodian of the bidden lore, (மறை, the Veda) he was the guard an of the sacred fire, the source of material prosperity to the state ; he was the person who performed the sacrifices according to the difficult orthodox rites, and who brought timely rain,

These are the terms in which these heterodox writers refer to him. He had a function in society and he discharged it faithfully. The whole attitude both of the orthodox and also of the heterodox, in matters religious, was the pity of the one for the ignorance of the other; but nothing more bitter, as Max Muller has very well pointed out.

Animism seems to have played an important part in the religious system of those days. There was a temple consecrated to the 'Chaste Lady' (Pattini Devi), as she was called, who died in consequence of the murder of her husband. Her images are preserved in temples up to the present times for, according to Dr. A.K. Kumarasami,[18] some of the images depicted in illustration of the ancient art of Ceylon are of this deified women. Sati was in vogue, but under well recognised limitations. This was permitted only to woman, who had neither natural guardians to fall back upon, nor children to bring up. That it was not uncommon for young women to

[18] J.R.A.S. 1909, p. 292.

return to their parents widowed is vouched for by a comparison that a poet institutes between the approach of darkness and the return of the widowed young woman, whose husband had lately fallen in war. Annual festivals were celebrated with great éclat, and one of the grandest was that to Indra celebrated at Puhar. I have gathered my facts from a vast body of Tamil literature only recently made available to the student. I now proceed to consider the sources of the information, which are the classical writers, Indian literature, Tamil and Sanskrit, and the Ceylonese chronicle. Of the first group, Strabo wrote in the reigns of Augustus and Tiberius; Pliny published his geography in A.D. 77; the Periplus of the Erythræanean Sea was written in the first century A.D. probably A.D. 60 but not later than A.D. 80; Ptolemy wrote his geography about A.D. 150; the Peutingerian Tables were composed in A.D. 222. There were other writers who wrote later, but we are not concerned with them directly. I would draw attention to three points, taken from the works of classical writers.

Pliny remarks : 'At the present-day voyages are made to India every year, and companies of archers are carried on board, because the Indian seas are infested by pirates'. Later on he says : 'It (Muziris) is not a desirable place of call, pirates being in the neighbourhood, who occupy a place called Nitrias ; and besides it is not well supplied with wares for traffic'. This was before A.D. 77. Ptolemy regarded this port Muziris as an emporium, and places the country of Aioi south of Bakarai. Though Ptolemy does mark the division of the Konkan coast extending northwards of Nitra (Nitrias of Pliny) and up to the port of Mandagara, which is identified with some place not yet definitely accepted in the southern Mahratta country north of Goa, as Ariake Andron Peiraton, meaning the Ariaka of the pirates in his time, says no more of pirates at all ; meaning there was no piracy, &c. The Periplus on the contrary does make mention of the piratic character of this coast and gives a straightforward account of its active prevalence at the time in regard to the ports in the neighbourhood. The bearing of this we shall see presently.[19] The *Peutingerian Tables* state clearly that two Roman

[19] The following account from Marco Polo of this coast is worth noting:

"There go forth every year more than a hundred corsair vessels on cruise. These pirates take with them their wives and children, and stay out the whole summer. Their method is to join in fleets of 20 or 30 of these pirate vessels together, and then they form what they call a sea cordon, that is, they drop off till there is an interval of 5 or 6 miles between ship and ship, so that they cover something like a hundred miles of sea, and no merchant ship can escape them. For when any one corsair sights a vessel a signal is made by fire or smoke, and then the whole of them make for this, and seize the merchants and plunder them. After they have plundered them they let them go, saying, 'Go along with you and get more gain, and that mayhap will fall to us also!' But now the merchants are aware of this, and go so well manned and armed, and with such great ships, that they don't fear the corsairs. Still mishaps do befall them at times."

He also notes in respect of the kingdom of Ely the following:—

"If any ship enters their estuary and anchors there, having been bound for some other port, they seize her and plunder the cargo. For they say, 'You were bound for somewhere else, and 'tis God has sent you hither to us, so we have a right to all your goods.' And they think it is no sin to act thus. And this naughty custom prevails all over the provinces of India, to wit, that if a

cohorts were maintained in the same town for the protection of Roman commerce.

Mr. Sewell, who has made an elaborate study of the Roman coins found in India, considers that an examination of the coin-finds lead to the following conclusions :[20]

1. There was hardly any commerce between Rome and India during the Consulate.

With Augustus began an intercourse which, enabling the Romans to obtain oriental luxu-

ship is driven by stress of weather into some other port than that to which it was bound, it was sure to be plundered. But if a ship came bound originally to the place, they receive it with all honor and give it due protection."

It would be interesting to note as Yule remarks that it was in this neighbourhood that Ibn Batuta fell into the hands of pirates and was 'stripped to the very drawers.' That region continued to be piratical up to the days of Clive and Watson as we know. In the days of Sivaji it continued to be piratical also, as he is said to have replied to an English embassy protesting against this piracy that "it was against the laws of Conchon" "to restore any ship or goods that were driven ashore." The central Asian ambassador Abd-er-Razzak has something to say of pirates near the Calicut coast.

Marco. Polo : Yule and Cordier (3rd Edn.) III Chap. XXIV and XXV. pp. 385-392.

20 J.R.A.S., 1904. p. 591.

ries during the early days of the empire, culminated about the time of Nero, who died A.D. 68.

3. From this time forward the trade declined till the date of Caracalla, A.D. 217.

4. From the date of Caracalla it almost entirely ceased.

5. It revived again, though slightly, under the Byzantine emperors.

He also infers that the trade under the early emperors was in luxuries; under the later ones in industrial products, and under the Byzantines the commerce was with the south-west coast only, and not with the interior. He differs from those who find an explanation of this fluctuation in the political and social condition of India itself, and the facilities or their absence for navigating the seas; and considers that the cause is to be sought for in the political and social condition of Rome.

From an examination of the second class of my sources of information alone, we find that there was a period when South India was under great rulers, who gave the country peace and thus provided the indispensable security for commerce. This period can be shown to correspond to that of the Roman empire from Augustus to Caracalla. After this period, we find the country in a condition of political flux. So then we may still find one, at least, of the most potent causes of this commercial decline in the internal condition of India itself. Pliny and Ptolemy do not mention the Roman cohorts at Muziris which the *Peutingerian Tables* do. The first exploit of the Red Chera's father is the destruction of the Kadambu[21] tree on the sea coast. Another compliment that the poets never miss an opportunity of bestowing upon this Red-Chera himself is that the Chera fleet sailed on the waters of that littoral with a sense of dominion and security. The Kaḍambu mentioned above is

21 (1) பலர் மொசிந்தோம் பியதிரள் பூங்கடம்பின்
கடியுடை முழு முதறுமியவேய்.

II. 11. ll. 12-13.

(2) கடம்பு முதறடிந்த கடுஞ்சின வேந்தே.

II. 12 l. 3.

(3) இரங்கு பிசிருடைய மாக்கடனீக்கிக்
கடம்பறு த்தியற்றிய வலம் படுவியன்பணை.

II. 17. ll. 5-6.

explained as a tree of extraordinary power which could not be cut down by ordinary man. I rather think from the context that it has reference to a piratical rendezvous of the tribe of people who became known as the Kadambas later. This view seems to be directly countenanced by the extract 3 on the last page which says in effect that he crossed the sea, destroyed the Kaḍambu and brought his enemies to subjection to him.[22] If this view be correct, the advent of the said Chera brought along with it security. This would be in conformity with Ptolemy's reference to Aay, who was one of the seven chieftains known to literature as 'the last seven patrons'. From the body of works known to Tamil scholars as Śangam works their contemporaneity could easily be established. I have examined this question elsewhere (in the Appendix on The Augustan

[22] It would be nothing surprising if the Kaḍambu tree, the country-date or some tree like it had been the tree-totem of this tribe. One tree in particular might have been regarded as peculiarly sacred by the tribe like the famous Oak at Dodona of the ancient Greeks or the slightly less famous Oak trunk of the Saxons of the days of Charlemagne.

Age of Tamil Literature), and find the name Aay a distinctive name of two individuals, and not quite of a family. The Aay must have been the contemporary of, or a little older than, Ptolemy, and the age of Ptolemy would practically be the age of the Red-Chera, and the Chera ascendancy. This conclusion only confirms what has been arrived at independently of this class of evidence. Gajabāhu of Ceylon, who visited the Red-Chera almost at the end of his reign, ruled according to the Ceylonese chronicle from A. D. 113 to 135. Allowing for the difference between the Ceylonese date of the Nirvana of the Buddha, and that arrived at by modern scholars, as Dr. Fleet, namely sixty years, that date for Gajabāhu would be A. D. 173 to 193. The Chera ascendancy then would cover the latter two-thirds of the second century A.D. Here has to be brought in the Paisachi work Brihat Kathā. Among the temples mentioned as having been found at Puhar was one dedicated to Sātavāhana. This personage was the ruler in whose court flourished the minister Gunādya, who was the author of this stupendous work which stands at the root of all romantic literature in India, whether in Sanskrit or any vernacular, and may be of the rest of the world as well. It was a translation of this work that set the fashion in Tamil for the composition of the romantic epics. The age of the original is still matter under investigation. The latest authority on the question is the Dutch scholar Speyer, who would place it in the third century A. D. at the earliest a date clearly impossible according to our line of inquiry. I shall not say more about it here now; but only remark that one of the works clearly based upon this, has to be referred to a period anterior to the astronomer, Varāhamihira A. D. 533. This work, MANIMĒKHALA refers to the asterism under which the Buddha was born as the fourteenth; which according to the modern computation, following Varāhamihira, ought to be the seventeenth. The Ceylon Chronicle also deserves to be investigated more carefully. So far investigations from different points of view only appear to confirm its chronology, except for the possible correction made above.

The date of the death of Caracalla corresponds closely to the disappearance of the Sātavāhanas of the Dekhan. According to the latest opinion the power of the Kushanas also vanished about the same period. In South India likewise the Pāṇḍya ascendancy passes into darkness. The century following is one of the dark spots in Indian History, until the rise of the Guptas in the north of the Chālukyas in the Dekhan, and of the Pallavas in the south.

Before closing, I may refer to the conclusions of a scholar, T. C. Evans, who has studied the India of this period in a thesis, Greek and Roman India, contributed to the Anglo-American Magazine for 1901. He concludes that "The Greek invader found there an ancient and highly organised society differing little in its usages and modes of living from those which exist at the present time; and although there are no means of verifying the conjecture, it is not unlikely that the population of the peninsula was as great in that period as in our own." Commenting on this, my friend Mr. W.H. Schoff of the Philadelphia

Commercial Museum makes the following remarks: "If this view is correct, India was the most populous region of the world at the time of the Periplus, as it was the most cultivated, the most active, industrial and commercial, the most highly organised socially, *the most wretched in the poverty of its teaming millions* and *the least powerful politically.*" He further follows that "the economic status of the country made it impossible that any one of these should possess political foree commensurate with its population, resources and industries. It was made up of village communities, and organised military power only so far as they were compelled to do so; and they were relatively unconcerned in the dynastic changes, except to note the change in their oppressors." While there is a great deal that is just in these remarks, some of them fail to take note of the time, and the circumstances, on which we are passing judgment from our twentieth century standard of political justice. The very extent of the country and the necessarily inferior character of the communications would make any other organisation than that of the village communities inefficient in the extreme. It is true perhaps that they had not the military power necessary for all time; but such as it was it often proved at any rate equal to the strain imposed upon it, often by successfully defending the country against foreigners. After all there is the possibility of a difference of ideal in organisation. A society essentially organised for peace and its requirements is certainly defectively organised for purposes of war. If the Hindu society at any time had been organised on any basis, it certainly was on the basis of peace and the happiness of the bulk of the people. It is this ideal that has the merit as well as the defect of Hindu organisations throughout the history of India. It is not difficult to understand by a comparison of the organisation of the British Empire at the present time which can be looked upon as having been made on an economic basis, with that of the German empire, which, at any rate, recent history shows to have been organised upon a basis for war. It ought rather to be said to the credit of the early Hindus that they regarded war so far an abnormal state of affairs that they had to provide for it only in an exceptional sort of way, and this is evident both in their organisation for peace, and in that of war, as far as it is possible for us to make out from the material available to us. About the very time of the Periplus, the Tamilian rulers of the West coast were quite able to hold their own as against the Greeks on the sea, and, though finally vanquished, it was the Punjab armies that made a very good stand against Alexander. Chandragupta could even lay claim to a victory against the most redoubtable of Alexander's generals. These instances ought to make us pause before accepting sweeping statements either as to military incapacity or to unfairly uneven distribution of property in the organisation of Indian society. I may quote here an address that a poet made to a king, a particularly warlike one, on the ideals that he ought to set before him at a time when there was perhaps some need for war. Here is a literal translation of the passage as far as a beautiful Tamil poem could be rendered into English prose. "Like the single eye that adorns the Majestic crescent face of Śiva, who, with Mount Meru for his bow, the great serpent for its string, destroyed the triple fortifications of the Rākshasas to give victory to the valiant host of the Devas, O Mara, of the flower garland! Great among Kings; great though your army may count, elephants of high mettle, horses of exceeding fleetness, high cars with tall flags and valiant soldiers eager for war, remember the Majesty of a monarch lies foremost in his walking the path of rectitude. Therefore may you be blessed with long life, without swerving ever so little from the path of rectitude because the people concerned are ours; without in the least discounting the good found in those not of us; may your valour shine with the brilliance of the sun. May your power of protection show in it all the beneficent coolness of the moon. May your charity be as seasonal and impartial as that of the rain itself. With the three great virtues just mentioned may your days count more than the sands of the sea washed ashore by the winds, on the coast of Śendil (Tiruchendur) where stands the great Kumāra." It would only be fair to the ancients to give them the ordinary credit of their having honestly attempted to pursue the ideal they set before themselves.

CHAPTER IV.

THE CHRONOLOGY OF THE ŚANGAM WORKS, SO CALLED, OF TAMIL LITERATURE

THIS subject has been, for very near a century, regarded as of the utmost importance by those engaged in research work as well as by those engaged in the study of Tamil, the eldest among the sisterhood of languages known commonly as the Dravidian languages. In the early years of the last century Bishop Caldwell made what perhaps was then the most successful attempt at fixing the age of this body of literature and brought what he called 'the Augustan Age of Tamil Literature' to the 9th or 10th century of the Christian era. Since then there have been a series of attempts several of them merely re-stating Caldwell's conclusions; while various others were made to controvert them and give a higher antiquity to this Augustan Age. The recent editors of

Caldwell's Comparative Grammar allow the following statement to remain: — "The Period of the predominance of Jainas (the predominance in intellect and learning give rarely a predominance in political power) was the Augustan Age of Tamil literature, the period when the Madura College, a literary association, appears to have flourished and when the Kuṛal, Chintāmaṇi, and classical vocabularies and grammars written."[1] This period is ascribed to the 9th or 10th century A.D. and the editors are content to leave this with a foot note: "Modern researches point to a much earlier date than that given here." This Caldwellian tradition has been handed on almost unbroken to the present time. We find the statement repeated with hardly any modification in Reinhold Rost's article on Tamil, in the 11th edition of the Encyclopædia Britannica; and with some slight modification

[1] What ever else may be proved or no, this old classification, by religion, of periods either of literature or art must be given up as it finds no support of any kind to justify its being kept up.

in Frazer's "A Literary History of India" and the new edition of the Imperial Gazetteer Volume, II. This position did not go unchallenged, however. It was the late Mr. P. Sundaram Pillai of Trivandrum who took up the challenge first. In one or two essays that he contributed on this particular subject he did much destructive work, but did not essay in constructive work, relating to this particular period, though it must be said to his credit that he succeeded in fixing, one or two milestones in Tamil Literature. The greatest constructive effort was made by another lamented Tamil scholar, the late Mr. Kanakasabhai Pillai, whose work, however, was marred by a too ambitious attempt at working out details before the main lines could hardly be regarded as fixed. This defect notwithstanding, his work brought together a great deal of matter which had remained buried in manuscripts inaccessible even to the learned, and understood, if accessible, by but a few. This work was done by him in the last decade of the last century and in the first two or three years of the present. It was about the end of this scholar's work that a much respected European Scholar, connected intimately with Madras, both as occupying an honoured place upon the High Court bench, and holding the position of the Vice-Chancellorship of our University, took up the question and restated the case in support of Caldwell's theory with much force, considerable learning and great judgment. This was the late Mr. L. C. Innes who discussed the whole question of the various periods of Tamil literature in what was then the Imperial and Asiatic Quarterly Review, in an article entitled the Age of Māṇikkavāśagar. One small identification in it in the fixing of this Augustan Age drew my attention to this particular investigation and I raised by no means a respectful protest against it in a short article which I contributed to the Christian College Magazine. The letter that he wrote in reply to this protest, of which I sent him a printed copy, led me on, thanks to the stimulus of that judicial minded good man to, make an effort at fixing this Augustan Age from my point of view. "The Augustan Age of Tamil Literature" was written by me in the first instance for the Madras Review and published, again in a somewhat modified form, in the Indian Antiquary as a general introduction to a contemplated series of articles on "Celebrities in Tamil Literature," poets and patrons alike. This was again published, with permission, by the Tamilian Archæological Society in the Tamil Antiquary. The essay attempted to set forth the then available evidence both literary and historical leading to the following conclusions:—

(1) "That there was an age of great literary activity in Tamil to warrant the existence of a body like the traditional Śangam".

(2) "That the period of the greatest Śangam activity was the age when Śeṅguṭṭuvan Sera was a prominent character in South Indian politics".

(3) "That this age of Śeṅguṭṭuvan was the second century of the Christian era."

(4) "That these conclusions find support in what is known of the later history of South India.

Since this was published there have been to my knowledge two constructive efforts of which one is that contained in a life of Śeṅguṭṭuvan in Tamil written by Pandit M. Ragava Aiyangar of the Tamil Lexicon Office, read in the first instance as an essay before the Tamil Śangam at its meeting in Ramnad in May 1913. The other is a final statement, of various efforts in detail in regard to this matter by Mr. Subramaniya Iyer, Assistant Epigraphist to the Government of Madras, in the Christian College Magazine of the year 1914, in an article entitled the Ancient History of the Pāṇḍya Country. I propose attempting to examine the position of these two scholars and restate my case in the light of the criticism thus made to see how far my position has to be revised and to what extent it requires to be altered.

Taking the latter first the point that calls for attention is that he relies, for settling this much disputed chronology, on a few copper plate grants of the Pāṇḍya Kings, and one or two stone inscriptions relating to them, and hopes from these aids to settle the question finally. The following long extracts from his paper would exhibit his position in respect of the others who had carried on similar investigations before him most fairly to himself.

'As has been remarked already the dates when these poems were composed are not given anywhere. To settle this question with any amount of probability, we are naturally forced to look for information from external sources. Even in this direction, there was not much to help us till recently. The discovery of the Sinnamanur plates and the information supplied in the Veḷvikuḍi grant of the Pāṇḍya kings have placed a lot of reliable matter before the earnest student of ancient history and a careful examination of their contents is sure to enable him to arrive at a satisfactory solution which has all along been sought for in vain. The previous scarcity of materials served only to mislead inquirers [2].

'For purposes of history we can freely adopt the accounts given in Puranānūru, Pattup-

[2] A fuller Examination of these follows in Ch. vii

pāṭṭu, Padirruppattu, etc. These poems have been edited in an admirable way by Mahāmahōpādyāya V. Swaminathier who gives now and then short notices of Aham which has not yet appeared in print. Although Śilappadikāram and Maṇimēkhalai are classed among the Śangam works, I entertain serious doubts as to whether they speak of contemporary kings and events, and it may be said that great caution is necessary before utilising wholesale the materials contained in them. I know *I am mortally wounding the feelings of several savants of Tamil literature who would at once pour forth a volume of abuse if I were considered a worthy rival of theirs.* Fortunately I am not such a one. But all the same I wish to record here my reasons for holding the position. The two works in question contain a romantic account of a certain Kaṇṇagi famed for chastity and of Maṇimēkhalā the daughter of a hetaira of Kannagi's husband Kōvalan. Enraged at an unreasonable murder of her husband, Kaṇṇagi miraculously sets fire to the city of Madura, whereupon the Pandya king struck down by remorse for the unjust act *kills himself.*[3] A heavenly palanquin is seen to descend to earth to carry Kannagi to the abode of the gods. The people who observed this, erect a shrine for her worship and this is at once followed by the initiation of the same worship in other countries both in and out of India. The romantic nature of the story will not fail to strike any one at the very outset. I for one would not grant that it relates to contemporary events. On the other hand it would be natural to view the legend as a story spun out by the poets, if not wholly from their imagination, at least with liberal addition to traditional beliefs extant at the time, of events long past. Is it possible, I ask, that a person, however virtuous he or she may be, would be invested with divinity even at the very moment of death? In my opinion, which I think will be shared by many, the story of the person should have remained in the memory of the people for a long time before any halo of

3 The poet merely says he died upon the throne where he was seated at the time.

divinity could gather round it [4]. It passes one's comprehension to imagine that people should have set about erecting a temple for a heroine at or soon after the time of her death.

'I ask further how long it would have taken for her fame not only to spread but to strike such deep root in other countries as to cause her image to be enshrined in costly temples. In this connection I would request the reader to bear in mind that she was neither a royal personage nor a religious prophetess. In all probability, if the story is due to a development of events taken from life, it must have been written long after Kannagi had been deified. As such we cannot assume the contemporaneousness of the kings mentioned in these works with the date of their composition.

[4] History does record various instances of canonization of ordinary people in Europe while yet alive. Augustus was deified during life and history knows that there was a temple to him in India on the West Coast where Kannagi had her first shrine. Ptolemy II and his sister-wife were given a similar apotheosis during life by their loving but perhaps superstitiously credulous subjects.

My own view is that the authors, not knowing the time when the kings mentioned by them individually flourished, have treated persons belonging to different ages as contemporaries and thus brought together a Gajabāhu, a Neduñjeḻiyan and a Karikāla as living at the same time. In my articles on the date and times of the last two kings, I have adduced reasons to prove that they must have lived at least a century apart. And I would further point out here that Mr. Kanakasabhai Pillai's identification of *Nūrranganṉan* mentioned in the Śilappadikāram with Śātakarṇi is entirely untenable, because there is no warrant for the reading Sātakarṇi of the name Śātakarṇi which we find in all inscriptions and coins. Though attempts at translating proper names are not quite uncommon, yet it would seem that in this case *Nūrranganṉan* is not a translation of Satakarni. If the Tamil name was the result of perfect translation, we should have expected Nūṟṟangādan instead. No foreigner has ever dealt with proper names in this fashion. We have the mention of Indian kings and geographical places by Greek and Roman writers and by the Chinese pilgrims who visited India. I may note that none of them has adopted the novel method [5]. And again it is a wonder that a similar attempt at translation was not made in the case of the other name Gajabāhu into Yānaikkai. [6] I would further state that if you examine carefully the contents of Maṇimēkhalai, you find mentioned in this work, assigned to the second century A. D., systems of belief and philosophy that could not have struck root till the eighth and ninth centuries.

'The Hon. Dewan Bahadur L. D. Swamikannu Pillai very kindly furnishes the following note on the question of the date of Śilappadikāram and Chintāmani :—

"As regards the date of composition of Śilappadikāram I have found that the details given by Aḍiyārkunallār in நாடுகாண்காதை and the prophecy about "ஆடித்திங்கள் ஆரிருள்பக்கத்து-

5 Is this true? What does Phrūriou stand for in Ptolemy's Geography of the Coromandel Coast?

6 What about ஓவிய சேனன் (Oviasēna) for Chitrāsena in this very author?

அழல்சேர் குட்டத் தட்டமி ஞான்று-வெள்ளிவாரத்து," etc., are satisfied in only one year between A. D. 1 and A.D. 1300, *i.e.*, A.D. 756. Similarly I have quite recently found that the details given in Jivakachintamaṇi in காந்தருவத்தத்தை-யாரிலம்பகம் (text regarding the Muhūrtam for construction of கானக்கிடங்கு and commentary by Nachchinārkiniyar on the 1st verse) are correct for only one year, A.D. 813.

"In either case the actual composition of the poems may have followed the respective dates by 60 to 80 years, the ordinary period for which Panchāngams are preserved [7]. My view is that the poets could have obtained the details only from a contemporary Panchānga, if indeed they did not find the details in the materials used by them for the poems. In the case of Jivakachintāmani there were materials on hand.

"The interval between this composition of சிலப்பதிகாரம் and சீவகசிந்தாமணி was only about 60 or 70 years or at most about 150 years, not 700 years as supposed by Kanakasabhai Pillai and others".

[7] If a Panchangam was used for the purpose.

'We can safely accept Mr. Swamikannu Pillai's date, A. D. 756, [8] for Śilappadikāram. Still, we cannot but maintain that the matter contained in this and other works of a similar nature is useless for purposes of history. If we are asked to explain further why we adopt the accounts furnished in Puṛanānuṛu and Pattuppāṭṭu as come down to us from the hand of Perundēvanar,—an author who cannot be said to have lived earlier than the date (A. D. 756) assigned to Śilappadikāram—we would say that Perundēvanār stands in the high position of an editor of some older and trustworthy *historical documents of great merit*, [9] while the authors of Śilappadikāram and other similar works appear before us *as mere story tellers and that their compositions are full of improbabilities, impossibilities and inconsistencies.*' *The italics are ours.*

The first point in the extracts to call for a word by way of remark is that the twin-epic,

[8] This is not his date. His date is 60 or 70 years later, according to him.

[9] How are these historical? Were they written to hand down history?

Śilappadhikāram and Maṇimēkhalai, is not to be used for purposes of history. He sets forth the reasons very elaborately thus:

(1) He ascribes to the authors of the books an ignorance of contemporary rulers, and sees in the combination of a Gajabāhu, a Neḍum-śeḻiyan and a Karikāla a confusion of chronology.

(2) He further refers to Mr. Kanakasabhai's identification of Śātakarni with "Nūrran-gaṇṇan" as unwarranted.

(3) He next sets down that the work Maṇimēkhalai contains reference to systems of belief and philosophy that could not have struck root till the 8th and the 9th centuries.

(4) And lastly he quotes Mr. Swamikannu Pillai, with approval, to point out that the Śilappadhikāram could have been composed only in A. D. 756, slightly overstating his authority.

In regard to the first point it may be stated at once that there is no immutable psychological law that prevents contemporaries from believing in the supernatural. In discussing the mental attitude of people separated many centuries from us it is a natural error to import our ideas into their lives. The first essential to a study of this kind is an attitude of mind that can detach itself from its present outlook and carry itself back to another environment. If we are inclined to regard the story of Kaṇṇaki as "improbable, impossible and inconsistent" it does not necessarily follow that our ancestors, perhaps 13 or 14 hundred years ago, on Mr. Subramaniya Ayyar's own showing, had the same mental outlook as we have. Even so we cannot say of us to-day that there are not among us people who will not believe stories similar to those of the Śilappadhikāram in contemporary life, and it is hardly fair in any one to ascribe to those with whom he does not agree that they make use of the works under consideration in the manner suggested by this remark. Nor does it make it necessary that the author should have lived centuries after the occurrence to share this belief. Granting for argument that he did not share the belief himself, but took up a story that was current and dealt with it in the manner that he has done, but laying the scene in the contemporary Tamil India of his time, the author would still be within the bounds fixed by literary criticism to a poet. All that is claimed for the two books is that the background of the story is historical, and those that have used it so have more to support them than their critics. We shall consider the contemporaneity of the rulers mentioned in the work later.

In regard to the next point it is not clear where the expression Nūṟṟangaṇṇan comes from. Mr. Kanakasabhai has attempted to identify the Śātakarṇi of the Śilappadhikāram with the expression Nūṟṟuvar Kannar or merely Kannar, but of "Nūṟṟangaṇṇan" I am unable to see any reference either in Mr. Kanakasabhai's book or in the Śilappadhikāram. It may be stated, however, that Mr. Kanakasabhai's identification is hardly tenable on altogether other grounds. We do not agree with Mr. Subramaniya Ayyar that if one name happens to be translated for some reason (*e. g.*, Oviasenan [ஓவியசேனன்] for Chitrasena) though we may not know it, it does not follow that others should be.

In respect of the third point of his, one would wish to know the grounds upon which a general statement like that is put forward. What are the systems in Maṇimēkhalai that could not have come in before the 8th or the 9th century and why? Where do these systems go back for authority and in what form is it that the systems are found exhibited in the Maṅimēkhalai? These points ought to be cleared before a general statement like that will be accepted.

In regard to the last point, the astronomical data that Mr. Swamikannu Pillai relies on are found in the work but imperfectly expressed. They are elaborated by the commentator who lived many centuries later than the author. It is more than doubtful if the author took up a *panchāngam* to set down the date or to note its details. It strikes me that he noted a particularly inauspicious combination for a day, such as the popular கேட்டை, மூட்டை, செவ்வாய்க்கிழமை, portending a coming storm of a violently destructive character. There is nothing to warrant that anything more was meant in the astrological details than this. Whether that is sufficient to override all other considerations in ascribing particular dates to works seems to me exceedingly doubtful.

Going to the more constructive part of Mr. Subramaniya Ayyar's work we are face to face with four inscriptions, namely.

(1) The Madras Museum plates of Jaṭilavarman,

(2) The smaller Śinnamanūr plates.

(3) The larger Śinnamanūr plates.

(4) The Vēḷvikuḍi grant.

His whole system depends upon a series of identifications of the various persons referred to in these four grants. We should invite attention particularly to the identification of No. 2 in the genealogical table constructed from the larger Śinnamanūr plates. This person's name occurs merely as Jaṭila, the equivalent of the Tamil Saḍaiyan, with no other detail to lead us to an identification. Mr. Ayyar has identified him with a Jaṭila whose name is found in the Anaimalai inscriptions which are dated 770 A. D. This person is again equated with the last name in the Vēḷvikuḍi grant which is itself undated, thus giving to this last person, the donor of the grant, the date A. D. 770. What is more, a minister, by name Mārankāri, whose name figures in the Ānaimalai inscriptions, is described, in the Sanscrit portion as mudurakavi, maduratara and sastravid, and as a native of Karavandapuram. This minister Mr. Subramaniya Ayyar takes to be definitely the Vishṇava Ālvār, Madurakavi, neglecting the caution with which the possibility of identification is advanced by both the late Mr. Venkayya[10] and Mr. G. Venkoba Rao the publisher of the Anamalai inscriptions. On this identification rests the whole chronology of Mr. Subramaniya Ayyar's thesis. These identifications and the various grants have reference only to the Pāndyas. The identification of Māran-kāri with Madurakavi seems almost impossible. If the tradition regarding Madurakavi is accepted for one thing, it ought to be accepted for other things equally essential. Madurakavi is by common tradition a Brahman and a native of

10 See Epigraphist's Reports for 1907 and 1908.

Kōlūr, and is not handed down, in Vaishṇava tradition at any rate, as an official of the importance that Māran-kāri was. There is nothing in the ten stanzas ascribed to Madurakavi to indicate that he was anything more than a pious devotee. On such a basis of identification and combination of the four records Mr. Subramaniya Ayyar constructs a genealogical table beginning with Palyāga-śālai Mudukuḍumi Peruvaḷudi [11] and ending with Rājasimha, taken to be a contemporary of the Chola Parāntaka I A. D. 907 to 956, on the ground that the latter's inscriptions state that he won a victory over a Pāṇḍya by name Rājasimha, which name unfortunately occurs twice in the larger Śinnamanūr plates themselves, with three generations between them. It will be clear from this how valueless would be the inferences based upon these grants which on Mr. Subramaniya Ayyar's own showing were composed in the 8th, 9th and 10th centuries, in regard to matters relating

11 Whose name, by the way, is brought into this grant to justify the name Velvikkuḍi and establish a prior gift of the village without any organic connection. For further details see Ch. vi-ii following.

to even two or three centuries earlier at the very worst.

Immediately after the first name Palyāga-śālai Pāṇḍyan, the Vēḷvikuḍi grant mentions a Kaḷabhra Inter-regnum. This Kaḷabhra Inter-regnum is taken to be an Inter-regnum brought on by a Karnāṭaka invasion, referred to in connection with the story of Mūrti-nāyanār in the Periyapuraṇam. Fixing up then a Pandya succession he proceeds next to enumerate 13 Pandya Kings whose names occur in Tamil literature, and tries to identify the later ten with those mentioned in the grants, and ascribes to them dates ranging from the commencement of the 6th century A. D. to A. D. 650 which he makes the terminal date for Śḻiyam Śēndan whom he identifies with the Neḍuṁ Śeḻiyan, the victor of Talaiyālangānam. This makes the whole course of identification simplicity itself. But there is however one grave difficulty in accepting this arrangement. The whole body of works called Śangam works which have to do with these various Pāṇḍyas have not the slightest reference to the Pallavas. Still 500 to 650, at any rate the latter half of it, was the age of the great Pallavas and 650 would take us perhaps to the middle period of one of the greatest among the great Pallavas, Narasimha I, destroyer of Vātāpi, the burning of which is referred to in the Periyapurāṇam. Sambandar refers to the Pallava general who destroyed Vātāpi. It is very strange that the large body of poets that went about from court to court singing the praises of patrons, and received rewards from them have no reference to make of the Pallavas although several towns and forts and territories under Pallava rule come in largely for reference. This objection seems vital to this chronology arrangement, and seems thoroughly to exemplify the defects of specialistic research of which Mr. Stanley A. Cook has the following remarks to make, in his "Study of Religions."

"The man who is specialistic in a single department may be a bar to progress because he is apt to overlook the importance of other special studies. His own convictions are the more intense when he associates them with his trained knowledge, and although he may realize that his own energy has brought him to this stage, and although he may recognize in some special field the need for other men of diverse types and tendencies, he may forget that it takes all kinds of people to make a world. The desire to promulgate and proselytize is characteristic of all men with strong convictions based on experience and knowledge, and they can be intolerant of others. *In research, social reform and religion, there is a stage of development, born of an intense feeling of the completest equilibrium or harmony in one's world of thought that can manifest itself in impatience towards, or in a provoking superiority over, those who differ.* Yet one must not deny to others that sense of harmony that has been gained by one's own efforts along one's own lines; and since the whole world of thought could be theoretically divided into numerous departments, the ideal in view is a harmonious adjustment of them all.'

Passing on now to Pandit Ragava Ayyangar's work, called Śēran Śenguṭṭuvan, in Tamil, we find him devote Chapter XIII of the book to the determination of the age in which Śenguṭṭuvan and his contemporaries flourished. Passing in rapid review the late Mr. Kanakasabhai's conclusion in regard to the matter, he lays down his main position somewhat as follows :—

It is well known that among the poets that constituted the Śangam, Kapilar, Paranar, Nakkīrar, Māmūlanār and Śāttanār took a prominent place. Among these Māmūlanār appears, from certain poems included in the Ahanānūru, to have been contemporary with Chola Karikāla, Śeralādan, Kaḷvar Kōmān Pulli ; from this source also appears clearly that he was one who had travelled much in the various parts of the Tamil country and in countries north of it. This poet is taken to be contemporary with Śenguṭṭuvan Śēra, as he refers, in Aham 251, to a war between the Mauryas and a chief of Mohūr which is taken to stand for the chief Paḻayan Māran who is said elsewhere to have fought against this Chera. Quoting from Aham 265, [12]

12 'பல்புகழ் நிறைந்த வெல்போர் நந்தர்-சீர்மிகு பாடலிக் குழீஇக் கங்கை-நீர்முதற் கரந்த நிதியங் கொல்லோ.'

he refers Māmūlanār to a time subsequent to the destruction of Pāṭalipura to which he sees a definite reference in the passage quoted. This is the first and in fact the strongest argument of his thesis for ascribing Śenguṭṭuvan to the 5th century A.D.; but he arrives at this result by a series of arguments which seem to me to find no justification in history. He interprets the expressions in the passage quoted as referring to the destruction of Pāṭalipura by the Ganges; whereas in actual fact it could mean no more than the disappearance of the great wealth that the Nandas collected in Pāṭalipura, in the Ganges. This might well have been brought about by the Nandas themselves throwing it into the river, rather than let it fall into the hands of their enemies, in the revolution that subverted their dynasty. Starting from his peculiar interpretation of the passage he postulates the destruction of Pāṭalipura by the flood of the Ganges and finds the period of such destruction in the time intervening the visits of the two Chinese travellers to India, namely, Fa Hian in the beginning of the 5th century and Hiuen Tsang in the second quarter of the 7th century A. D. He further equates the Mauryas who had invaded the territory of Paḻayan Māran, perhaps in a previous generation, with the army of the Gupta King, Samudra Gupta-He finds support for this in the mention of the Maṇṭarāja who is taken to be 'a King of Kerala' and the same as Māndaram Śēral. The rest of his reasoning in the whole Chapter is of the same character and of minor consequence. Granting for the sake of argument that his interpretation of the passage quoted above is correct, it would be very difficult to justify Samudra Gupta and his army being referred to as Mauryas by a poet of the standing and reputation of Māmūlanār. There is absolutely nothing in the pillar inscription [13] of Samudra

13 Kauśālaka-Māhēndra-Mahā kāntāraka-Vyāghra-raja-Kaurājāka--Maṅṭarāja--Paishṭāpuraka-- Māhēndra-giri Kauṭṭūraka Svāmidatta-Airāṇḍapallaka--Damana-Kānchēyaka-Vishnugōp-Āvamuktaka.

Nīlarāja--Vaingēyaka—Hastivarmma—Pālakkak—Ograsēna---Daivarāshṭraka--Kubēra--Kausthalāpuraka--Dhānanjayaprabhriti sarvva-dakshiṇāpatharāja-grahaṇa-mōksh-ānugraha-janita-pratāp-ōnmiśra-mahābhāgyasya-

Gupta to warrant this inference. The text of the inscription contains reference to a Kauraḷaka Maṅṭarāja. He is mentioned along with Hastivarman of Vengi, Vishṇugopa of Kānchi, Ugrasēna of Pālaka etc. There is absolutely nothing in the inscription to lead us to believe that Samudragupta's army passed south of Kānchi. That that Maṅṭarāja should be taken to be Māndaram Śēral is identification of the most unreasonable kind. The editor of the inscription, Dr. Fleet, did not understand what the term Kaurāḷaka stood for, and merely put forward a suggestion that it might be " Kairāḷaka" the equivalant of "of Kerala". This suggestion is in a foot note, but as to the point whether the person referred to was a Kerala prince at all he has offered no definite support. It has since been found that Kaurāḷaka is very probably a mere mislection for Kauṇāḷaka (of Kuṇāla) perhaps the region round Kollēr lake.[14] But whatever it is, it is now certain that there is no reference whatsoever to Kerala

14 Epigraphia Indica Vol. VI, p. 3 note by the late Prof. Kiebhorn.

in the inscription. As to the destruction of Pāṭalipura by flood there is no authority for the statement. The recent investigations on the site seem more to indicate a certain amount of destruction by fire very much more than by water, and the passage relied on cannot be held to support the interpretation put upon it. After all if one of the poems of Māmūlār makes reference in the past tense to the destruction of Pāṭali or to an invasion of the south by the Mauryas and a war in consequence between them and one of the Tamil chiefs of Mōhūr (near Madura) this can only mean that Māmūlanār knew of these occurrences. The various passages of Māmūlanār, most of which are unfortunately in the Aham, will hardly serve to establish his contemporaneity with all the incidents he might have found occasion to mention. The identification of Tadiyan with Tidiyan, and of Pidiyan with Paḷayan borders on the ludicrous. There is a further reference to the Jain work Digambara Darśana, (ascribed to the 10th century, and to a statement in it as to the establishment of a Drāvida Śangam in Madura by

Vajranandi in A. D. 470 (Samvat 526). There is nothing to prove that this was a Tamil Śangam for the fostering of Tamil Literature. It may well be a Jain Sangam which would, in the sense of being an assembly of Drāviḍa Jains or Tamil Jains, be a Drāviḍa Śangam and may have had for its object some matter pertaining to the Jain religion. Thus then the elaborate reasoning exhibited in Chapter XIII of the work seems clearly to rest upon a very uncertain and slender basis. It is regrettable that a book which does exhibit considerable labour and puts in an eminently readable form matter buried in recondit works should be marred by this kind of reasoning, particularly in this Chapter and in Chapter VIII [2] where he tries to establish that the Vanji of the Cheras was the Karur in the Trichinopoly District, where again we come upon a number of distortions of texts and a number of false identifications to establish his thesis.

The proper procedure in a case like this is to analyse the various works belonging to this particular group, sort out the various kinds of historical evidence that we get, establish the undoubted contemporaneity of poets and patrons with a jealously critical eye, and look out for historical connections that will establish one or more synchronisms, and proceed on that basis to establish others.

Adopting this procedure the Śangam works so called fall naturally into two classes:—Those dealing, according to the Tamil grammarians, with (1) Ahappōruḷ, and (2) Purapporul. The distinction between these two broadly is that the one refers to subjective emotion which finds expression on various occasions and under various circumstances, and has reference principally to Erotics; the other refers to action and partakes more or less of the character of exhibition of valour in attack, defence and the various other aspects of war-like life. Of these two classes the latter is the more valuable for purposes of history and chronology, as it makes direct reference to various wars, battles, sieges etc.; and one very special feature of such work is that poets composing in this strain always address their patrons directly, thereby making it unmistakable that what they have to state in respect of a particular chieftain has reference to contemporary life. The other group, however, does not stand on an altogether similar footing. Poems in this group do make similar references though they are always of an indirect character and do not give such clear evidence of contemporaneity in respect of their various statements. These works are Puṟananuṟu, Ahanauru, Pattuppattu, Padirruppatu, Aingurūnuru, Narrinai, Kuṟuntokai, etc. [15]. I keep out from this group advisedly the two works Śilappadhikāram and Maṇimėkhalai to which I shall return later to see how far the almost contemptuous reference to them of Mr. Subramaniya Ayyar finds jurisdiction. Even so the number of poets and patrons that figure in the works are far too many to be dealt with in one thesis. I shall take occasion to

[15] Of these all but the second have been edited in an excellent form, the larger number by the veteran Pandit Saminatha Iyer, but the last two are edited by two others whose labours deserve as much credit as the other's. Naṟṟinai was published by the late Mr, Narainasami Iyer of Kumbhakonam and Kuṟuntokai by Pandit Rangasami Aiyangar of the Madrasa at Vaniambady.

deal with these more elaborately, and on a scale compatible with the degree of lucidity that a lay understanding would demand of necessity. I can do here nothing more than to illustrate the work to be done by one or two typical examples of a telling character. In taking up a question like this a student of research is pretty much in the position of a judge and not of an advocate. Feeling and sentiment are out of the question and the discovery of truth is the object in view. There are here as in the case of a judge the two questions coming up for examination: questions of fact, and questions of law. One has to examine facts before stating them as such; one has to examine the method that he adopts in the choice of his facts as much as in their application. Bearing this in mind we have first of all to consider whether stone inscriptions and copper plate grants are better authority for events which could have taken place centuries before the inditing of these documents or literature that was composed ostensibly at the time to which they relate. These Śangam works enumerated above are, by common consent, such works of contemporary value and have therefore to be regarded as of better authority. Mr. Subramania Ayyar takes Perundēvanār as of high standing and authority in respect of these works because he was a cultivated scholar and responsible editor of these, though coming centuries after their composition. But he forgets this, at any rate he seems to, in claiming a similar kind of authority for the compilers of the inscriptions which he seems unmistakably to set over against this class of literature to the disadvantage of the latter. Taking the poet Paranar to exemplify this position and collecting together such facts as we could derive from him of an undoubtedly historical character, we can find the political condition of the Tamil land and the position of the Tamil chieftains in relation to one another, in the poet's generation.

In stanza 4 of Puranānūru, Paraṇar refers to a Chola ruler Uruvapahrērilanjētchenni in the following terms: they are of the radiant beauty of the rising sun just emerging out of the sea, in his golden car of the fullest effulgence.' This king is known from other poems of the same class, but of other poets, to be the father of Karikāla. The terms in which Paranar chose to describe him in this poem raise the presump tion that he was the ruler, Tigaloḷinãyirrēḷpari neduṁtēr Chola, the grandfather of Śenguṭṭu van Śera; but this is by the way. Poem 63 of the same collection relates that the chera king, Kuḍakko Neḍum Śēralādan, and the chola king, Vērpaharaḍakkai Peruvirarkkiḷḷi, had fought against each other and fallen on the field of battle. Another poet Kaḷāttalaiyar has also celebrated the same king, in the same connection. Poems 141 and 142 both refer to Pēhan's liberality which is referred to by the somewhat later Nallūr Nattan, the author of Siṛupaṇaṛṛuppadai. Poems 144 and 145 are addressed to this chief when he had given up his wife in favour of a sweetheart. Paranar, Kapilar, Ariśil Kilār and Perunguṅṛur Kiḷār interceded in behalf of the wife to good purpose. Such a reference as we get in these two poems is an absolutely unmistakable evidence of contemporaneity[16]. Poem 343 refers to Muzires

16 Compare Aham 148 at "Kāṭṭūr Tāyangaṇṇan."

(Muśiri or Muyiri) and states, in regard to it, that commodities brought oversea were brought ashore by means of boats. The place was full of goods brought overland and from across the sea to be distributed among those in need, that might go there. Narrinai 6 of the same author has a reference to Ōri 'of the good bow.' In Aham 396, Śeṅguṭṭuvan is celebrated, while there are references in the poem to the war around Nannan's Paḻi hill-fort and to Mignili. There is further reference to the story of Adi Mandi and Āttanatti, and possibly to the defeat of Ori. The poem also appears to be intended to celebrate the imprinting of the bow emblem of the Chera on the Himalayas. Poem 62 of Aham, as also poem 208, refer to the famous Kollippāvai having been erected by the gods. He later also refers to the war with Mignili round Paḻi hill. It must be noted in this connection that the tradition regarding Kollippavai is found very clearly recorded in the following poem of Ahananuṟu by another author known as Kallāḍanar who refers in the same poem to Pandyan Nedum Śeḻiyan, victor at Talaiyālanganam. There is similar reference to another chieftain Pulli, (robber-chieftain, of the Tirupati hills. There is also a statement that Kāri, king of Mullūr, killed Ōri and made over his territory round Kollimalais to the Chera King. Poem 270 of Narrinai refers to the story that Nannan captured the elephants of his enemy as well as their women folk, binding the elephants with ropes made out of the hair of the women, cut off for the purpose. Poem 73 of Kuṛundokai has a very interesting reference to a class of warlike people called Kōśar who entered Nannan's territory after killing his state elephant. This warlike tribe of people are referred to in other poems of the same class, and almost in the same terms. One of them referring to their being 'men of united counsel' capable of hurling the irresistible "battering-ram". These are, in other poems, associated with Kongu, and are referred to as Kongu Ilangōśar in the Silappadhikaram. Kuṛundokai 292 gives in detail the story that Nannan killed a girl for having eaten a fruit that had fallen from one of the trees in his garden into a stream of running water and was being carried down by it. He would not accept the ransom offered of 9 times 9 elephants and a golden statue of the girl of her own weight. It must be said to the honour of the Tamils that his name was handed down to posterity branded "as Nannan the woman-killer." Aham 147 of the same author states that Aay Eyinan, known as the commander-in-chief of the Chera, fought with Mignili and fell in the fight. Poem 152 has reference to Veḷiyan Tittan and his port known as Perunduṛai, and what looks a naval defeat of another chieftain Pindan in this place. There are allusions to Pāḻi hill and Naḻḻi. Aham 165 refers to the Kōśar 'of united counsel,' and seems to refer to their location in Kongu. It also contains the names Anni and Mignili but the passage is too corrupt to know the connection fully. Aham 372 refers to the capture of Tirukkovilūr, the capital of Kāri by Adiyamān of Tagaḍūr. That Paraṇar celebrated this incident is stated in plain terms by Avvaiyar, the poetess, in poem 99 of Puṛanānūru.

From these references collected in this fashion we could form a more or less definite picture of the political divisions of the Tamil land in the generation of Paranar. This picture becomes very much more definite and clear, if we could collate it with similar imperfect pictures that we may form by a study of other single authors such as Paraṇar himself. We shall reserve that for a future occasion. Now taking Paraṇar alone we find him celebrate the Chola who was father of Karikāla definitely as a contemporary, as also Śēramān Neḍum Śēralādan and the Chola Vērpahaṟaḍakkai Peṟuvirarkkiḷḷi. This chola probably was either the father of Karikala or his grandfather. We find this Paraṇar celebrating Śēran Śenguṭṭuvan in the fifth section of the Padirrupattu. We have already made reference to this author's direct reference to Adiyamān, Pēhan, Nannan, Kāri and others. These must therefore have come all in one generation, that is, the generation extending from the grand-father of Karikāla to the Chera Śenguṭṭuvan. The period of time ascribed to any one of these chiefs must be a period that would fit in with this political condition of the Tamil land. It has already been pointed out that this somewhat vague picture of the political condition of the South is capable of being completed by bringing into collation the picture that can be made of it from other authors whose works have come down to us like those of Paraṇar. Without going elaborately into that comparison I may at once state that the Tamil land was divided among the three kings: the Pāṇḍya with his capital at Madura, the Chera with his capital at Vanji on the west coast, and the Chola with his capital at Uraiyur,[17] at the commencement of this generation. The intervening region and the border land of the north where a good deal of fight would have to be done was divided among a number of chiefs who were very often independent of the kings and sometimes acknowledged allegiance to one or other of them. Of such we find mention in the writings of Paranar himself. The information that we obtain from him is confirmed and supplemented by venerable poets among

[17] Abam 31. வென்றியொடு—வில்லலைத்துண்ணும் வல்லாண் வாழ்க்கை—தமிழ் கெழுமூவர்காக்கும்—மொழி பெயர் தேஎத்த பன்மலை யிறந்தே.

whom mention may be made of Mamulanār from whom I have to draw for further information later on. It is this latter that makes mention of Pulikat as the Vaḍuka frontier (northern frontier)[18]. The corresponding frontier on the western side seems to have extended to the north of the Tuḷu country into which, as was noticed already a new tribe with the name Kosar effected entry in the days of Nannan[19]. Immediately to the east of them were the territories of the two chiefs Vichchikkōn and Irungoveḷ of Araiyam, just below this and along the hill region bordering the western Ghats and the Eastern where they meet the Western was perhaps the chieftain Pāri of Parambunāḍu. To the east of it was the territory of Adiyamān of Tagaḍūr (Modern Dharmapuri), to the south east of which was the territory of the chieftain Ori with his territory round about the Kolli-

18 Kur. 11 குல்லைக்கண்ணி வடுகர்முனையது.வல்வேற் காட்டினன்னாட்டும்பர்.

19 Aham 15 மெய்ம்மலி பெரும்பூட்கோசர்-தோகை காவிற் றுளுநாட்டன்ன.

Kur. 73. நன்னனுமா—கொன்று நாட்டிற் போக்கிய—வொன்றுமொழிக் கோசர்போல

malais. Across into the South Arcot District, particularly the hilly portions of the west, was the territory of Kāri with his capital Tirukōvilūr. Behind them, almost in a sort of second line, was the chieftain Pēhan with his territory round the Palnis; Aay round the Podiyil hill in the Madura and Tinnevelly districts; Evvi on the Coromandal coast with his territory embracing a part of the Pudukkōtta state and the District of Ramnāḍ. There is another chief the Tonḍaimān Iḷandirayan who was certainly the contemporary of Avvai and Adiyaman Anji, though not directly mentioned by Paranar. His Capital was at Kanchi and he ruled the territory round Kanchi under Chola suzerainty. We have besides to locate, from the works of Paraṇar himself, the Kōśar somewhere in the Kongu country. This seems the political distribution of the territory belonging properly to the Tamil land in the generation of Parañar the poet. Any age therefore that could be ascribed to the Sangam, in which Paranar did play a prominent part, must exhibit more or less this condition of political distribution of territory in the Tamil country. Any age which, from what could be known of it, does not visualise this political division has therefore necessarily to be rejected. The question therefore now is whether the latter half of the 6th and the first half of the 7th century, fixed by Mr. Subramaniya Ayyar, or the 5th century to which Mr. Ragava Ayyangar assigns the Śangam, fit in with the political circumstances thus shadowed forth from the works of Paraṇar. The first alternative is very easily disposed of. The period of a century from 560 to 650 was the period when the great Pallavas were prominent political factors in the south, and practically the whole of the Tamil country was under their influence in the northern half. The southern enclave was equally indisputably in the hands of the Pāṇḍyas among whom the most prominent character was the famous Kūn Pāṇḍyan or Sundara Pāṇḍya or Niṅṛaśir Neḍumāran. His contemporary of the north was Narasimhavarman I, Pallavamalla. Both of them had for their contemporaries alike the Tēvaram Hymners, Appar and Sambandar. There is no reflection of this political condition in the literature under examination, nor is there any prominent mention of the Pallavas at all, in the region where they held, sway, about which however, Paraṅar has a very large number of references to make. While these literary men take the greatest pains always to distinguish one ruler from another of the same dynasty by giving to each the distinguishing epithet, it is not open to us to identify, without sufficient lead from our sources, one ruler with another without very substantial reasons. The identification of Śēndan Seḷiyan of the copper plates with the Pandyan NeḍumŚeḹiyan of Talaiyālangānam fame is, to say the least, not proven. In regard to the historical value of the Śilappadhikaram and Maṇimēkhalai about which a few words must be said here by way of reply to Mr. Subramaniya Ayyar's contemptuous reference, which betokens an amount of ignorance which would be inexcusable in one with any pretensions to scholarship. Śenguṭṭuvan Śēra figures prominently in both the works. The author of the first is the younger brother of Śenguṭṭuvan. The author of the other is his friend and both of them worked at a subject, legendary or other, that caught their imagination and dealt with it poetically, laying the scene, however, in the contemporary Tamil India of their time. Now the question is: Are we to accept the statement of this prince-poet when he speaks of his parentage or not, though he might choose to put it, as a poet, in the mouth of one under a spell? Are we not to accept his statement in regard to the achievements of his brother particularly when they happen to be confirmed in every detail by an independent poet Paraṇar who celebrates him in one section of another work Padiṟṟupattu? Those that have taken it upon themselves to use these poems know their responsibility obviously, and use the material presumably with critical care. It is just possible that there are differences of opinion in respect of a detail here or a detail there as being of a historical character or no. But a wholesale condemnation such as is found in the extract from Mr. Subramaniya Ayyar quoted above, can be but the offspring of blank ignorance and incapacity to appreciate other mental attitudes and situations.

Passing on now to the other period so far ascribed, the Pandit is perhaps on a little more safe ground, but the arguments with which he finds it necessary to buttress this position shows its weakness. I need only mention two points here: (1) The erroneous and impossible identification of Maṅṭarāja of Kurāḷa with Mandaramśērāl of Kēraḷa which name, by the way, does not find mention to my knowledge in these works. (2) The equation of the Vambamōriyar with the army of invasion under Samudragupta. It has already been pointed out that the interpretation of the quotation regarding the Nandas is wrong altogether, and that it is so is proved by a similar passage in lines 4 and 5 of poem 251 of Aham[20]; but there are a number of references which carry the invasion of Mauryas up to Mōhūr of Paḻayan Māran. In one of these passages at any rate, the Pandit tries to establish the contemporaneity of this invasion with the Paḻayan Māran, which, from the text, is untenable. The term Mōhūr is used in the

20 அருந்துயர் கேட்பின்-நந்தன் வெறுக்கை யெய்தினும் மற்றவட்டங்கலர் வாழி தோழி. Compare note 10, S. 89 ante.

passage to stand for the chieftain of Mōhūr not necessarily Paḻayan Māran. That reference and the various other references to the Mauryas in Māmūlanār, as well as the reference to their cutting their way through rock in their march southwards, all of them do refer possibly to a great southward invasion[21] of the Mauryas, a newly-established dynasty. We know now beyond doubt, since the discovery of the new edict of Asoka at Maski in the Nizam's dominions, that Asoka's territory extended right down to the frontier of Mysore within the boundaries of which other edicts were discovered years ago. We know of no wars excepting the famous Kalinga war that Asoka carried on for purposes of conquest. Chandragupta not having had the time to do it, the further conquest of territories not included within his Empire but included within that of his grand-son, historians ascribe to Chandragupta's son Bindusara, the father of Asoka who himself held the

21 Aham 69 & 281. மோரியர் seems the preferable reading in Puram 175. The blundering of the commentator is worth remarking.

viceroyalty of the southern frontiers with his capital at Vidiśa (Bilsa)[22]. The conquest of the south by the Mauryas must have therefore been made either by Bindusāra the king, or, by the viceroy-prince, his son. The term Vaḍukar used in this connection by the Tamils is a general designation for all northerners, and indicates, in the various references before us, an onward move southwards of certain northern tribes of which we get perhaps the final glimpse in the movements of the Pallavas till they come into occupation of Kanchi and the extension of their power at least as far south as Trichinopoly and Kumbhakonam. All the passages of Māmūlaṇār, referring to these incidents, refer to them as past occurrences and not as contemporary events. This interpretation of the passages relating to northerners agrees very well with the claim of certain Tamil kings to having won victories over the Aryan army, which attribute is specifically given to the

22 V.A. Smith's Early History of India (3rd edition) p. 149. Notice the footnote containing the statement of Tāranātha, the Tibetan historian.

Pāṇḍyan Neḍum Seḷiyan whose name figures in the Silappadhikāram. Such a general movement against the north could on general considerations be postulated only of the period of confusion that followed the decline of Maurya power in the north and the rise, to the imperial position afterwards, of the Andhras and the Andhrabhrityas in succession. The fifth century is hardly the century in which we get anything like a glimpse of such a great movement of people. With this general position of affairs clearly before us, the Gajabāhu synchronism does not appear in the least impossible; but appears on the contrary very highly probable. The information that could be gathered from the Ceylon Chronicle Mahāvaṁśa compiled in its present form in the 6th century, but from material put together in epic form at the commencement of the 4th century, from a written source traceable to the first century B.C., is not as unreliable as it is too readily taken to be. If that Buddhist chronicle does not refer to Pattinidēvi in so many plain words we have no right to expect it; but that does not invalidate the existence of a Gajabāhu or of his visit to the court of Śenguṭṭuvan Śēra.[23] The synchronism thus established must, it seems to me, stand; no satisfactory reason having been put forward so far to invalidate it. The newer information only goes so far to confirm it. The tradition of Pattini has taken such a hold upon the people of Ceylon that it is quite likely it was introduced under the favourable auspices inferable from the Śilappadhikāram, though naturally the Buddhist chronicle of the Mahāvihāra omits mention of it [24].

23 It must be noted, however, that other chronicles, which may reach back to similar old sources, do mention the incident specifically. (Vide Upham's—Rajaratnācari & Rājāvaḷi)

24 Indian Antiquary. XLV pp. 72-78.

CHAPTER V.

THE AGE OF PARANAR

IT will be noticed from what has been said in relation to the condition of Indian civilization at the dawn of the Christian Era that the information put together has been drawn from various sources which have been merely indicated in the course of the narration. It would be worthwhile classifying and arranging these sources with a view to investigating what exactly the relative value of each of these sources would be in respect of the particular period to which that general account has reference. Some of these sources have already been explained in sufficient fullness to indicate their value such as the Dipavamśa and the Mahavamśa, the chronicle accounts of Buddhist Ceylon.[1] We have also indicated in the course of the chapters II & III the relative value of the classical writers; and

[1] Vide chaps. 1 & 2 *ante*.

the Sanskrit writers who make any reference to South India have been examined in some detail in chapter I and their value estimated.

Coming down to inscriptions and epigraphical matter generally, it may be said that the material available for work for this period, is so little that we might assume that the epigraphical material other than the legends on coins is perhaps as good as absent, except for the Asoka inscriptions and just a few others in regard to this part of India. There is left then the literary sources, of which both Tamil and Sanskrit, and various Sanskritic languages could be exploited usefully. But for this period even Sanskrit and Sanskritic languages are of comparatively minor importance to classical Tamil literature, and that we shall take into consideration just now.

In order the best to understand the value of this literature and appraise it at its real worth, let us see a little more closely what exactly we can find in relation to the particular authors or particular generations of authors, and having projected from such information as is available, a picture from these sources alone, we might then so far compare that with what may be available, to check the accuracy of it, from the other external sources to establish the correctness of the picture already drawn of South India at the beginning of the Christian Era. To do this, we shall take a poet known to readers of classical Tamil as Paranar.

Paranar was one of those traditional 49 literary men who constituted the third academy of Madura. His name is of peculiar importance in Tamil literature as it connects itself with the names of certain well-known celebrities in that literature, and in consequence we could gather round his name certain well-known figures. Moreover, he seems to have been a long lived man and his generation takes in a pretty long series of rulers and poets. By studying him we can gain something like a full idea of what the south India of his days was. Paranar is regarded traditionally as a Brahman. His writings occur in a large number of the Tamil classics known collectively as Śangam literature. He is a poet who sang of the Chera Śenguttuvan, whose name is connected at once with the Śangam classics on the one side, and with the twin-epic Śilappadikāram-Maṇimēkalai which, it has recently been contended should be regarded as something quite apart from the former, and separated from them by a comparatively wide interval of time. It will be clear even to the lay reader if Paranar sang of Śenguṭṭuvan, as he does in the fifth book of the Padiṛṛuppattu, and if Śenguṭṭuvan's younger brother was the author of the Śilappadikāram, and his friend, Śāttan the author of the Manimēkalai, then the age of all of these must be one and the same whatever that age might be. Of Paranar's works we have twelve short pieces in the collection Naṛṛiṇai, fifteen poems in the Kuṛuntogai, one ten of the ten-tens (Padiṛṛuppattu); thirty-two poems in the collection Ahānanūru and twelve in the Purānanūru, with one in the collection called Tiruvaḷḷuvamālai. And such a number would be considered voluminous work, and have a comparatively wide range in respect both of matter and manner. In Puram 4,[2] he

2 பொலந் தேர்மிசைப் பொலிவு தோன்றி
மாக்கட னிவந்தெழுதருஞ்
செஞ்ஞாயிற்றுக் கவினை மாதோ.
யனையை யாகன் மாறே. Paranar, Puram 4.

celebrates a Chola Uruvapahrer Iḷanjetchenni whose somewhat queer name seems to be derived from a comparison which this poet has instituted to him in the poem, under reference, where he is likened to the morning sun who in radiant majesty rises out of the sea in the glorious red of dawn. This Chola we know from the poem Porunarāṟṟuppaḍai of Muḍattāmakkaṇṇiyār, [3] was the father of the great Chola Karikāla. He celebrates in Puram 63 the Chera (Kuḍakko Neḍuṁśēra-lādan [4], and the Chola (Peruviraṟkkilli) when both had fought and fallen on the field of battle. This same event is celebrated by another poet who goes by the name Kaḻātta-laiyar [5]. One of the so called last seven patrons by name Pēhan whose territory was round the Palnis was celebrated by this poet. One of the references to him is in regard to his large beneficence without expectation of a reward [6]. One supreme instance of such being his

3 உருவப்பஃறேரிளை யோன்சிறுவன்.

4 Note at foot of the poem. Puram. 62.

5 Puram. 141 & 142.

6 Puram. 144 & 145.

providing a wild peacock with a cloak or mantle as a protection against cold. The second which is more to our point is his intercession in behalf of Pēhan's wife Kannaki (not the heroine of the Śilappadikāram) whom he had abandoned in favour of a courtesan. Paraṇar pursuaded him to walk in the path of rectitude by returning to his wife. On this same occasion in the same sad connection three other poets intervened in behalf of the abandoned wife. Their names are: Kapilar, Ariśil Kiḻār, and Perunguṅṛūr Kiḻār, authors respectively of the seventh, eighth, and nineth 'tens' of the 'ten-tens' collection. In Puram 369 there is reference according to the Colophon to the Śēramān Kaḍalōṭṭiya Vēl Keḻu Kuṭṭuvan (Kuṭṭavan Chera, who drove his enemies with his javelin on the sea) who must be regarded as identical with Śenguṭṭuvan of the Śilappadikāram, as Paraṇar refers to this latter in almost identical terms in poem 46 of the Padiṟṟuppattu [7]. In Narrinai six, he refers

7 பல் செருக்கடந்தகொல் களிற்றியானைக்
கோதைசால் பௌவங்கலங்கவேலிட்

to the chieftain Ori of the Kollimalais, and in stanza 201 of the same work he has reference to the famous statue of the goddess Kollipāvai. This poet also describes in some detail various transactions in connection with the chief Nannan of Konkan (Koṇkānam). Chief among this was the war that the Chera undertook against him. In the course of this war or in another, the Chera general called Āay Eyinan, the commander-in-chief of the Chera fell in battle against Nannan's commander-in-chief Gnimili [8]. He also refers to the accumulation of the vast wealth of Nannan in the citadal Pāḻi. One poem in Kuṟuntogai (292) gives in detail the story of Nannan's putting to death the girl that ate the fruit of Nannan's garden carried down stream in a canal through the

டுடைதிரைப்பரப்பிற்படு கடலோட்டிய
வெல் புகழ்குட்டுவன்.

ll. 11 to 13.

8 அடுபோர் ஞிமிலி செறுருவல்கடை இ
வண்மை யெயினன் வீழ்ந்தன்ன ஞாயிறு Aham 180.
கடும்பரிக்குதிரையா அயெயினன்
நெடுந்தேர் ஞிமிலியொடு பொருதுகளம் பட்டென

Aham. 147.

garden [9]. The savagery of this chieftain is again brought under reference in Naṟṟiṇai 270, where he is described as having shorn his enemies' women folk of their hair to make ropes of them for fastening captured elephants. Reference has already been made to Paraṇar's stating that a tribe of people, the Kośar, entered Nannan's territory after killing his state elephant. There are a number of allusions to several incidents in the life of Nannan. Another reference that must be noted here, as of some importance, is to the entry of the Kośar into Kongu in Ahaṁ 195 [10].

Returning now to the fifth-ten of the Padiṟṟupattu, where he celebrates Śenguṭṭuvan Chera, we find Śenguṭṭuvan Chera described in the Padikam (epilogue) as the son of Neduṁśēralādan "King of the westerners" by Manakkilli

9 மண்ணிய சென்ற வொண்ணுதலரிவை
புனறருபசுங்காய் தின்றதன் றப்பற்
கொன்பதிற் றொன்பதுகளிற் றொடவணிறை
பொன் செய் பாவை கொடுப்பவுங்கொள்ளான்
பெண் கொலை புரிந்தநன்னன் போல.

Kuruntogai 292.

10 ஒன்று மொழிக் கோசர்க்கொன்று முரண்போகிய
கடுந்தேர்த் திதியன் முங்கைதக் கொங்குழை.

a Chola Princess [11]. He is said first of all to have marched across forests up to the Ganges, defeating his enemies on the way for the purpose of a stone to make the statue of Pattini (the deified heroine Kaṇṇaki). He is also said to have returned from the expedition bringing in a vast number of heads of cattle belonging to his enemies. The next achievement of his is the utter defeat of his enemies at Viyalūr and the destruction of the place. Getting across to the other shore, he destroyed the fortifications of Koḍuhūr. He marched further into the territory of Paḷayan and having cut down his margosa tree (perhaps another totem) captured a number of his elephants and yoked them together by ropes made of the hair of the women folk of the enemies. His next exploit is the defeat and destruction of a number of Chola princes, collateral cousins of the reigning ruler, who carried on constant war for the time being outside Vāyil (Nērivāyil of other works). And last of all is the destruction of his enemies on the sea, which was already referred to in

11 She is called Naṟchōṇai in the Śilappadikāram.

connection with Puram 369. Of the various incidents found in this padikam (the epilogue of the poem) some of them are described in detail in the body of the poem itself. His northern invasion is described in general terms in lines 6 to 11 of poem 43 of the Padiṟṟup-pattu [12]. His invasion against the territory of Paḻayan and his allies, and what he is said to have done there in the course of this war are described in some fullness of detail in lines 10 to 17 of poem 44 [13]. There is a reference to his wearing 'the garland of seven crowns' in line 6 of poem 45 [14]. In poem 46, lines 11 to 14, there is a clear reference to his fight on the sea and the destruction of the protection that the sea offered to his enemies : obviously the pirates

12 கடவுணிலை இயகல்லோங்கு நெடுவரை
வடதிசை யெல்லை யிமயமாகத்
தென்னங் குமரியொடா யிடையரசர்
முரசுடைப் பெருஞ்சமந் ததையவார்ப்பெழச்
சொல்பல நாட்டைத் தொல்கவி னழித்தப்
போரடுதானைப் பொலந்தார் குட்டுவ

13 மோகூர் மன்னன் முரசங்கொண்டு
நெடுமொழி பணித்தவன் வேம்பு முதறடிந்து
முரசு செய்முரச்சிக் களிறுபல ஞிட்டி &c.

14 எழுமுடி மார்பின் எய்திய சேரல்.

who found their shelter in the sea [15]. In line 4 of stanza 48, he is described figuratively as a veritable fisherman [16], who constantly engaged himself on the sea to get rid of his enemies with a view to making the articles coming over sea, available to those inside his own territory. In poem 49 lines 7 to 10 and in lines 16 to 17, there is a reference again to the determined stand made by Paḷayan against this Chera and his final destruction [17]. The last of all in poem 50, line 7, there is an obvious reference to the junction of the three rivers Kauvery, Amravati, and Kudavanār [18] This

கொல் களிற்றியானைக்

15 கோடுநரல் பெளவங் கலங்கவேலிட்
டுடைதிரைப் பரப்பிற் படுகட லோட்டிய
வெல்புகழ் குட்டுவன்.

16 நீர் புக்குக்
கடலொடுழந்த பனித்துறைப் பரதவ

17 வெல் போர்வேந்தரும் வேளிரு மொன்று மொழிந்து
மொய்வளஞ் செருக்கி மொசிந்து வருமோ கூர்
வலம்படுகுழூ நிலையதிர மண்டி

....

கருஞ்சினைவிறல் வேம்பறுத்த
பெருஞ்சினக் குட்டுவற் கண்டனம்.

18 காவிரியன் றியும்பூவிரி புனலொரு
மூன்றுடன் கூடிய கூடல்.

last reference, I bring in here, as recently a great deal had been made of it to show that the capital of the Chera was Karoor on the Āmrāvati (Ān Porunai or Porundam.) As against this there is in this very poem itself a number of references to the perennial flow of water in his Periyār, which in one place at any rate is described as having its source in his territory and emptying itself into the sea in his own territory. (L. 13 to 18 of poem 48) [19]. Reference also might be made to line 15 of poem 43 [20]. The meaning of the reference to the three streams is obvious if one remembers that his uncle is said to have conquered the country of Kongu in line 15 to 16 of poem 22 of this collection [21].

Of these achievements, the Śilappadikāram describes elaborately his northern invasion

19 நின்மலைப் பிறந்து நின்கடல் மண்டு
மலிபுனல் நிகழ்தரும் தீநீர் விழவிற்
பொழில்வதி வேனிற் பேரெழில் வாழ்க்கை &c.

20 அருவியற்ற பெருவறற் காலையும்
மருஞ்செலன் பேராற் றிருங்கரை யுடைத்து &c.

21 மாகெழுகொங்கர் நாடகப்படுத்த
வேல்கெழுதானை வெருவரு தோன்றல்.

and makes clear reference to his having undertaken it for the purpose of bringing the stone and of the various details as to his victories against the northern enemies ; but how far the invasions were true is not exactly to our purpose at present. It is, however, a pity that there is not a reference to this pattini in those words in the body of the work apart from the epilogue. What is called a padikam or pāyiram in Tamil, an epilogue and a prologue respectively, is not to be added at any time and by everybody that chooses. It is generally of the nature of a preface, or a foreward, or a recommendation made by one more or less directly or intimately connected with the author. The only remote man who can do this is a commentator, but I believe not generally one who is separated very remotely from the author. In any case, the presumption of the statement being untrue would be unwarranted when we find all the other statements made in this piece are confirmed by reference to the body of the work. Even in respect of this particular it cannot be said that there is no reference as it is possible to read it in lines 6 to 11 of poem 43[22]. The others of them are repeated almost in the same words in at least two places in the Śilappadikārām by the anthor, who is no other than the younger brother of this Chera ruler himself.

There are however, in respect of these achievements two matters which call for special remark. His father claims victory over Kaḍambu of the sea in lines 13 and 14, of poem 11 [23]. There is reference to the same incident in line 3 of poem 12 [24], in lines 4 & 5 of poem 17 [25], and in lines 2 to 4 of poem 20 [26].

22 கடவுணிலைய கல்லோங்கு நெடுவரை
வடதிசை யெல்லையிமயமாகத்
தென்னங்குமரியொடாயிடையரசர்
முரசுடைப்பெருஞ்சமந்ததையவார்ப்பெழச்
சொல்பலநாட்டைத் தொல்கலனழித்த
போரடுதானைப் பொலந்தார்க்குட்டுவ.

23 பலர் மோசிந்தோம்பிய திரள்பூங்கடம்பின்
கடியுடை முழுமுதறுமியவேஎய்.

24 கடம்பு முதறடிந்த கடுஞ்சினவேந்தே.

25 துளங்குபிசிருடைய மாக்கடனீக்கிக்
கடம்பறுத்தியற்றிய வலம்படுவியன்பணை யாடுநர்.

26 எங்கோ
விருமுன்னீர்த்துருத்தி யுள்
முரணியோர்த்தலைச் சென்று
கடம் புமுதறடிந்த கடுஞ்சினமுன்ப
நெடுஞ்சேரலாதன் வாழ்கவவன்கண்ணி.

The last of these refers distinctly to an island of his enemies which may be of the nature of a delta. He is also credited with having imprinted his bow emblem on the Himalayas after having subdued the Āryas of the north. But, strangely enough he is also given credit in the padikam at the end of the second-ten of his having taken prisoners some Greeks (Yavanas), bound their hands behind their back as prisoners, and pouring ghee on their heads and taking what seems to be meant for heavy ranson for setting them free. It is the first achievement of his, which in another place the poet describes as giving him the primacy among rulers between the Himalayas and Cape Comorin, that gave him the name 'Imayavaramban' Neḍuṁśēralādan, the former word meaning he that had the Himalayas for his boundary. This expression, like a few others of the kind unfortunately, has been corrupted by the late Mr. Kanakasabhai Pillai into 'Imayavarman' for which there is absolutely no authority in the texts concerned. These incidents of the father are of some importance as the titles derived from these are applied to the son. The third ten of this work has reference to a younger brother of Imayavaramban, and therefore the uncle of Śenguṭṭuvan. He is given credit for having overthrown the fort of Ayirai (poem 21 line 29)[27]; he is given credit for having brought the Kongu Nāḍu under his control in lines 15-22 of poem. 23. Line 26[28] of the same poem gives him credit for having destroyed a hill fort somewhere. In lines 10 and 11 of poem 28[29] there is again a clear reference to the Periyār being the river of these Cheras. But of course the Periyār may be referred to generally as the great river, but in interpreting this, one ought not to forget the statement that he it was that brought the Kongu under his control and therefore the river of the Chera should be interpreted as having reference to a river in the Chera country proper and not in a later acquisition. It is this conquest of the Chera that has given him credit

27 கேருயர் நெடுவரையயிரைப் பொருந.

28 தண்ணைலம் பெருங்கோட்டகப்பா வெறிந்த.

29 பெருவறற் காலையு
நிவந்து கரையிழிதரு நனந்தலைப் பேரியாற்றுச்
சீருடைவியன்புலம் வாய்பரந்து மிகீஇய.

for having bathed in both the seas in one and the same day[30], which is only perhaps a somewhat exaggerated way of stating that in his time his territory touched both the eastern and western seas. So then we see that Śenguṭṭuvan who succeeded probably both his father and uncle became the heir to territory right across the whole of south India from the west coast in Cochin to somewhere across to the east coast through Kongu. Whatever the justification or otherwise, both the father Neḍuṁśēral and the son Śenguṭṭuvan lay claim to 'the garland of seven crowns', which could mean no more than what the Mummuḍi of the later times did mean, the three crowns and the seven crowns respectively, signifying the rulership of the three kingdoms and perhaps the seven kingdoms. This seven is not a mystic number. There seem to have been seven principal chieftains among whom the territory in south India was divided at the time, as we shall notice in another connection.

30 கருங்களிற்றியானைப்புணர் நிரை நீட்டி
இருகடனீரு மொருபகலாடி.
Padigam. to third ten of the Ten. Tens.

In this particular connection the historical character of these poems, cannot be called into question even by those who had the greatest objections to find historical matter in the twin-epic Śilappadikāram - Manimēkalai. But as against them this must be said that the authors of the twin-epic were one of them a brother, and the other a friend of Śenguṭṭuvan and what either of them has to say in the historical passages of the poem, which are easily distinguishable from the rest, find confirmation detail for detail in these poems which are very much more historical. All honest scepticisms therefore must accept as historical such personal touches as one finds even in romances. The real difficulty is the necessary critical faculty to distinguish what is historical in an unhistorical work. Śenguṭṭuvan Śera's father and uncle, therefore, were historical personages in whose reigns the western sea littoral of India was infested by pirates[31],

[31] This view of the term Kaḍamba in the poems finds strong confirmation in the City of Nannan having been known 'Kaḍambin peruvāyil' (*vide* Padigam in the fourth-

and both the father and the son exerted themselves untiringly to put an end to this piracy on their coast. That they did it with great success is in evidence in the various Tamil poems which describe the flourishing and very highly valuable trade of the ports of the west coast. Such a state of things both in regard to the piracy of the coast, and to its absence at a particular period, are in the clearest terms detailed in regard to Roman trade in the work of the classical geographers. It has already been pointed out that Pliny complains of this piracy; perhaps soon after Pliny got his information, the careful author of the Periplus makes mention of it, in the region opposite his Chersonesus.

ten poem. 40 ll. 13—15.): [1] ; and the Kaḍambar being one among four Kudies (cultivators) in Puram. 335 ll. 7 and 8. [2].

Kāppiyaṟṟukkāppiyanār on Kaḷangāykkaṇṇi nārmuḍichchēral.

1 பூழிநாட்டைப் படையெடுத்துத் தழீஇ
யுருள் பூங்கடம்பின் பெருவாயினன்னனை
நிலைச் செருவினாற்றலை யறுத்தவன்.

2 துடியன் பாணன் பறையன் கடம்பனென்
றின்னான் கல்லது குடியுமில்லை.

Māngudi Kilār.

He then proceeds to mention what he calls the White Island before coming down to Naura and Tyndis, the first markets of Damirica. The Chersonesus in the Periplus seems undoubtedly to refer to the tongue of land which makes a small peninsula at the mouth of the Kali Nadi as it is called in North Canara. Opposite to this is the cluster of islands called the 'Oyster Rocks' perhaps the Caenitae of the Periplus. White Island is the Lieuke of the geographers and is the same as the vernacular Veḷḷiyan Kallu or Tūvakkal, either of which is an exact translation of Lieuke or White Island. This is identified with Pigeon Island in the new Imperial Gazetteer[32] Then we come to the first ports of Damirica (Tamil country) and they are given as Naura and Tyndis corresponding to Nitras and Tyndis of Ptolemy. Ptolemy describes Nitras as a mart in the country, which he describes as Ariaka Andron Peiraton, that is the Ariaka of the pirates. It is of this Nitras that Pliny remarks that "ships frequenting the great emporium of Mouziris ran the risk of being

[32] Vol. 20 p. 136.

attacked by pirates, who infested the neighbourhood and possessed a place called Nitras. Thus Nitras figures both as a mart and as an island off the coast. This could only mean that the island was on the line of entry to the port of Nitras wherever that was. Nitras or Naura of Pliny is identified by Mr. Schoff with Cannanore which appears too far south. Cannanore, as has been already pointed out, is the Mont d'Ely of the mediæval geographers. Yule's guess that Nitras refers to Mangalore turns out correct. Mangalore is situated at the head of a delta formed by two rivers Nētravati and Gurupa. It is the Nītravati that has given the name Nitrias or Nitron or perhaps even Naura to the city. That may also have been the cause of the name of the island Nitron set over against the port. Tyndis is much farther south and has been identified with Kadalundi, not far from where Beypore is at present. Thus then we find the pirate coast of the Periplus to have been between Karwar point at the southern extremity of North Canara and the port of Mangalore. That answers exactly to the description that we get in early Tamil literature of the Kaḍark-Kaḍambu (the Kaḍamba pirates) having been found in the sea and having to be constantly defeated by war across the sea to their island-rendezvous by both the Chera Śenguṭṭuvan and his father. That would explain why Ptolemy has got absolutely nothing more to say of these pirates than the mere chracterization of the coast as the pirate coast. The Kaḍambas must have been a pirate race to begin with till they were re-claimed to civilization somewhat later perhaps. This conclusion is certainly in keeping with the position of the savage Nannan, the women-killer, whose capital is described, as already remarked, as Kaḍambin Peruvāyil, that is the large and the wide gate of the Kaḍamba country. He was after constant war put to death by another Chera celebrity Kaḷangāykkaṇṇi Nārmuḍi-ch-Chēral, the hero of the fourth 'ten' of the 'ten-tens.' Thus then it is clear that these poems of classical Tamil taken along with what is available in the Classical geographers makes it clear that the first Cheras known to history distinguished themselves in the southern opposition set up to the Aryan incursions from the north, and made conquests in south India so as to extend their territory from coast to coast across the peninsula. Their particular service however to civilization consisted in their suppression of this pest of piracy on the west coast which both the first Chera known to us and his son took so much pains to suppress, while other Cheras perhaps subordinate chieftains did make substantial contribution towards achieving this object. The period when this littoral was free from pirates extended approximately from A.D. 80 to A.D. 222, the date of Peutingerian Tables.

A study of the poems of Paraṇar with such of the available collateral material both literary and other leads to this knowledge which is found confirmed by two collateral lines of evidence extraneous to this literature: namely the information available from the classical geographers, and the results that could be drawn from the various finds of Roman coins along the coast of this part of the country; and these results might be set down as follows :-

Paraṇar has reference principally only to the Chola kings and the Chera kings. He does not appear to have celebrated the Pāṇḍya rulers very much. He has at any rate something to say of various chieftains who figure incidentally in his poems and the fact that recurs in respect of three or four Chera rulers and chieftains that they wore "the garland of the seven crowns" would refer to the seven chieftains known in Tamil literature as the seven last patrons of literature. The Chola kings are in order Peruviral Killi, his successor Ilanjet-Chenni, his successor Carikāla with an indirect reference to a number of Killis (Cholas) who fought in fratricidal war bringing on the active intervention of the great Red Chera (Śenguṭṭuvan). In regard to the Chera, he celebrates Imayavaramban Neḍum Śēral and his son Śenguṭṭuvan Śēra a younger brother of the first and another chieftain Nārmuḍi Chēral figuring as it were in between the two. We have certainly to bring in within the age of Paraṇar the chief Pēhan, otherwise called Vāyāvikkon-perum-Pēhan. The mention of the Chola and the Chera who fought and fell on the field of battle brings him into contemporaneity with another poet Kaḻāttaḻayār, who celebrated the same event. This latter poet is also stated in another poem by Kapilar to have destroyed the capital city Araiyam of Iṛungō Vēḷ by Kapilar whose elder contemporary he must have been.

In this connection we may consider a few references in Māmūlanār, the other poet to whose work we made reference already in a previous chapter. One reference of importance is in poem 55 Aham, which refers in specific terms to the battle of Veṇṇil where the Chola Karikāla defeated the contemporary Chera, who feeling ashamed of a wound on the back is stated to have committed suicide by starvation. This very same incident is referred to by two other poets Kaḻāttalaiyār and Veṇṇikkuyattiyār in almost the same specific terms respectively in Puram 65 and 66. While the first poet's reference may be considered somewhat indirect, that of the other two is quite direct and specific and is almost addressed straight to one of the combatants, the victor in this particular instance. This same poet Māmūlanār has in poem 126/27 of Aham a clear reference to the Cheras' achievement against the pirates and this may lead to the inference that the poet was contemporary with him. He refers to a Pāṇḍyan also but gives no specific indication as to which of the Pāṇḍyans it is. There is in the same work 232/33 a reference to the Chera who fed the hosts in the Bhārata war. What is more particularly to our point at present is the reference to a battle where Evvi, a chieftain of the Pāṇḍyan country, one among the seven patrons fell in battle. There he mentions the name of Paraṇar and brings him in connection with the fallen chief as having praised his valour, and that makes Evvi contemporary with Paraṇar. Another chief that is brought into contemporaneity with Paraṇar is the Adigaman Anji of Tagaḍur (Dharmapuri in the Salem District). This chief is said in poem 114 of Mamūlar to have been in hiding along with his relations out of fear of a chief who seems to be Nannan, if the reading of the text is correct. In poem 207, Paraṇar refers to the Kollimalais as belonging to Ōri, but in the next following poem however, another author by name Kallāḍan refers to the death of this Ōri. According to this, Ōri was put to death by Kāri of Tirukkoilur who made over Kolli to the Chera king. The allusion here is to a war or rather a series of wars perhaps of ambition. Anji of Tagaḍūr laid siege to Tirukkoilur of Kāri having defeated him in the field. Kāri not being able to make an effective stand against the enemy, went for protection to the Chera who was anxious to get possession of the Kollimalais. Kāri volunteered service, went across at the head of an army, defeated and killed Ōri and made over the territory round Kollimalais to the Chera. In the same poem this Kallāḍan refers to the battle Ālangānam where the "seven" were defeated by the Pāṇḍya. We shall refer to this later. Without proceeding further unnecessary length we might now take it that Paraṇar was acquainted with the chief Kāri, Ōri, and Evvi, among the famous seven, not to speak of the minor ones. We have already referred to his connection with Nannan. Thus then we come to a generation, Paraṇar's generation of poets and patrons, that gives us a number of Cheras and

Cholas in succession, as also the majority of the chiefs who go by the name the last 'seven patrons in Tamil literature.' We shall consider one or two other poets of the like eminence with Paraṇar and then say whether the postulating of a body called the third academy of Madura is warranted by this body of literature. By way of summary however, we might put it here that the Chola Karikāla, his father and grand-father were contemporaries with the Chera Neḍum Śēral and his father, perhaps also this Chera's son Śenguṭṭuvan. The chieftains are: Pēhan, Ōri, Kāri, Adigan, Evvi, Nannan and Āay-Eyinan. All these seem referable to the same age, that of the generation covered by Paraṇar. The poets that we have already come across are: Paraṇar himself, Māmūlanār, Kapilar, Ariśil Kiḻār, Perungunṟūr kiḻār, Kaḻāttalaiyār, Vennikkuyattiyār and Kallāḍanār, and these give promise of a complete academy itself. Though Paraṇar does not in so many words specifically refer to any particular Pāṇḍiyan, there is one reference which ought not to be passed over and that is in Aham 115. There is a battle referred to here at Kūḍarp-Parandalai. The first part Kūḍal would refer to Madura, the second part might be simply interpreted as a battle-field. In this battle the Pāṇḍya beat off from the place the two other kings who simultaneously attacked him and captured their war drums. This sounds very much like the war of the young Pāṇḍya king known in literature as victor at Talaiyālangānam, whose history we shall take up for consideration

CHAPTER VI.

THE AGE OF THE TALAIYALANGANAT-TUP-PANDYAN NEDUM'SELIYAN

I:—Sangam Literature.

This personage is a great Pāṇḍyan, one of the latest perhaps of the age we have taken for consideration. This complex name is composed of the general designation with a few modifying adjuncts. Śeḻiyan or Neḍuṁ-śeḻiyan may be considered his name. To distinguish him from others of that name, because this is a common enough name among the Pāṇḍyas, the attribute is added of his victory at Talaiyālangānam, identical probably with a village not far from the Niḍāmangalam Railway station in the Tanjore district. In that battle he is stated to have won a victory against a combination of all the kings and chieftains of the Tamil country. The fact that he is given this distinct epithet shows that, to the literary men of the age, there was no other battle of that name known, nor of a Pāṇḍyan who stood victorious.

To us this character is of the highest importance historically, because it seems to be he that comes into connection with the Pāṇḍyas of a later time specifically referable in inscriptions. From the poems it is clear he came to the throne of his fathers quite young. The neighbouring powers taking advantage of the new succession and of the youthfulness of the successor, marched with their allies, the five chieftains, and laid siege to Madura. It is then that the youthful monarch is stated to have made the poem 72 of Puram in which he said " they look ludicrous indeed [1] who saying that this ruler is young marched at the head

1 நகுதக்கனரே நாடுமீக்கூறுந
ரிளைய னிவனென வுளையக்கூறிப்
படுமணியிரட்டும் பாவடிப்பணைத்தா
ணெடுநல்யானையுந் தேருமாவும்
படையமை மறவருமுடையம் யாமென்
றுறுதுப்பஞ்சா துடல்சினஞ்செருக்கிச்
சிறுசொற் சொல்லிய சினங்கெழு வேந்தரை
யருஞ்சமஞ்சிதையத் தாக்கிமுரசமொ
டொருங்ககப்ப டேஎனாயிற் பொருந்திய
வென்னிழல் வாழ்நர் சென்னிழற்காணாது
கொடிய னெம்மிறையெனக் கண்ணீர்பரப்பிக்
குடிபழிதூற்றுங் கோலேனாகுக
வோங்கிய சிறப்பினுயர்ந்த கேள்வி

of their vast armies to the siege of my capital talking lightly of my prowess. If in this war I do not defeat their armies and capture all their war drums and themselves as prisoners, may my rule offer no protection to my subjects; may my subjects weep for lack of it, and blame me as an unworthy monarch; may the poets of my court with Māngudi Marudan cease to celebrate me in poems of praise." The same sentiment and the mean advantage that the other rulers took of his youth, and what they thought his helpless condition, are portrayed in the four next following poems by one poet who goes by the name Idaik-Kunrūr Kiḻār, who says in the first that the seven rulers marched upon the one king, Pāndya. He expresses surprise at the unusual sight of the whole body of 'seven' attacking the single ruler. In the following three poems he refers to the youth of the Pāndyan and of the attack

மாங்குடிமருதன் றலைவனாக
வுலகமொடுநிலைஇ யபலர் புகழ்சிறப்பிற்
புலவர் பாடாது வரைகவென்னிலவரை
புரப்போர் புன்கண்கூர
விரப்போர்க்கீயா வின்மையானுறவே.
The Pāndyan of Talaiyālangānam Puram 72.

being delivered upon his city wherefrom he beat the enemies off to their own territory and destroyed them there. That he was attacked outside his own city, is referred to in Aham 115 of Paraṇar.[2] It was this battle that was celebrated elaborately both in the Madurai Kānchi of Māṅguḍi Marudan, otherwise referred to as Māṅguḍi Kiḻār, and the poem Neḍunal Vāḍai of Narkīrar perhaps refers to the same campaign. The battle itself is very well described by this latter poet directly in Aham 36.[3] Of the poets

2 மையணியானை மறப்போர்ச் செழியன்
பொய்யாவிழவிற் கூடற்பறந்தலை
யுடனை ந் தெழுந்த விருபெருவேந்தர்
கடன் மருள் பெரும்படை கலங்கத்தாக்கி
யிரங்கிசை முரசமொழியப் பரந்தவ
ரோடு புறங்கண்ட ஞான்றை.

Paraṇar in Aham. 115.

3 கொய்சுவர்ப் புரவிக் கொடித்தேர்ச்
செழியனாலங்கானத்த தன்றலைசிவப்பச்
சேரல், செம்பியன், சினங்கெழுதிதியன்,
போர்வலியானைப் போல்ம்பூணெழினி,
காரறிநறவி னெருமையூரன்,
றேங்கழ் கலத்துப்புலர்ந்த சாந்தினி
ருங்கோவேண் மானியறேர்ப்பொருநன் (னென்.)
றெழுவர் நல்வலமடங்க வொருபகல்
முரசொடு வெண்குடைட (ய) கப்படுத்துரைசெல்க
கொன்றுகளம் வேட்டஞான்றை.

Narkkirar in Aham. 36.

that celebrated this great Pāṇḍyan, Māṅguḍi Marudan was perhaps the oldest and the most respected. Next follows the great poet and grammarian Narkīrar. Another one of equal eminence was Madurai Marudan Iḷanāgan, as he was called. Another important poet was Kallāḍan, besides Kuḍapulaviyanār, Iyūr Muḍavanār, Kārikkaṇṇan of Kaveripaṭam and Iḍaik-Kunṟūr Kiḻar.

This famous battle of history is described in some detail by Narkīrar who sets down, in Aham 36 already referred to, the combatants against him as Śéral, Śembian (Chola), Titiyan, Eḻini (son of the Adiyaman Anji of Tagaḍur), Erumaiyūrān, Irungō Vēṇmán, Tērpporunan. Aham 208 [4] of Kallāḍan refers to the battle of Ālangānām and speaks of the seven, referring in the same poem as an event of the past the capture of the Kollimalais by Kāri from

4 பொன்னணி நெடுந்தேர்த் தென்னர் கோமான்
எழுவுறழ் திணிதோளியறேர்ச் செழிய
னேரா வெழுவரடிப் படக்கடந்த
வாலங்கானத்தார்ப்பினும் பெரிதென.

Kallāḍan in Aham 208.

Ōri, and its gift to the Chera by the former [5]. Among these seven were the Chera and the Chola who are taken to be respectively the Chera Yanaik-kat-Chēy Māntaram Śēral Irumporai and the Chola Rajasūyam Viṭṭa Perunarkkiḷḷi, who together are celebrated by a poet by name Vaḍavaṇṇakkaṇ Perumjāttan though the two are not connected by name in the poem itself [6]. This defect is remedied to a great extent by the direct reference in Puram 17 of Kuruṅgōḷiyūr Kiḷār of the imprisonment of Yānaik-kat-Chēy by the superior force of the Pāṇḍya, who is clearly this Pāṇḍyan of Talaiyālangānam. [7] That this Chera chief is sometimes referred to with the attribute of the elephant-look is clearly explained in

5 முள்ளூர் மன்னன் கழறொடிக்காரி
செல்லாநல்லிசை நிறுத்தவல்வில்
லோரிக்கொன்று சேரலர்க்கீத்த
செவ்வாய்ப் பலவின் பயங்கெழுகொல்லி.

Ibid in Aham 208.

6 Puram 125.

7 ll. 20 and 21. read in connection with the comparison to elephant fallen into a pit. See also Commentary on p. 23 Mah. Swaminathaier's edition.

Puram 22.[8] Another poet Porundil Iḷaṇgiran celebrates this Chera of the elephant-look, and makes a very interesting reference in the course of the poem to a remark made by the Chera in respect of the older poet Kapilar, which gives us an idea of the age to which we shall have to allot this group of poets and patrons. The reference is "it were better that there was now alive Kapilar of illustrious name, whose skill in making poetry, and whose information on matters of importance, were unparalleled." The poet says that this remark was made by the prince himself and approves of it, following that if he were alive he would certainly set forth the praise of the Chera's country in suitable poetry.[9] The group

8 ஓங்கு கொல்லியோரடு பொருந
வேழ நோக்கின் விறல்வெஞ்சேய்

மாந்தரஞ் சேரலிரும்பொறை யோம்பியநாடே.

Kuruṅgōliyar Kilār in Puram 22.

9 செறுத்த செய்யுட் செய்ச் செந்நாவின்
வெறுத்த கேள்வி விளங்குபுகழ்க் கபில
னின்றுளனாயின் னன்றும னென்றநின்
னாடு கொள்வரிசைக் கொப்பப்
பாடுவன் மன்னாற் பகைவரைக் கடப்பே.

Porundil Iḷangiran in Puram 53.

therefore is to be referred to a time after the death of the poet Kapilar whom we have already referred to as a comparatively junior contemporary of Paraṇar.

This same conclusion is forced upon us by Narkīrar, another contemporary poet who celebrated elaborately this same Pāṇḍyan. In Aham 78, Narkīrar refers to Pāri of Parambunāḍu, the life-long friend of the elder poet Kapilar, who was at one time besieged by the three kings and some chiefs, and who being hard pressed for food in his citadel, employed parrots to fly out of the fort and bring in ears of corn for the use of the besieged on the advice of Kapilar. This is the last siege of Pāri's fortress and we know from Kapilar's history that Pāri fell in this siege and Kapilar went forward with the two daughters of Pāri thus orphaned to get them married properly. This brings Narkīrar into connection with Kapilar, as a younger and not perhaps very remote contemporary. In 253-52 there is a reference to the Pāṇḍya having driven away the Kongar, wherefrom is not exactly stated. In the same poem this Narkīrar refers to the chief Erumai and his country. In 290-89 of the same poet there is a flattering reference to a Chera and in 345 the Pāṇḍyan is said to have defeated the Chola in Kūḍal (Madura). The camp life of this Pāṇḍyan when he is out for war forms the theme of his poem Neḍunal Vaḍai, one of the Pattuppāṭṭu. We shall revert to this Narkīrar presently. But we may note in passing here, Puram 57, where a poet by name Kāri Kaṇṇan of Kaveripaṭṭanam exhorts the Pāṇḍya to desist under all circumstances, from cutting down what are called Guard-trees (Kaval-maram). What actually the poet says is, 'you may let your army plunder the standing crops of the enemy; you may let them set fire to their cities; you may kill enemy warriors, but see that you permit the destruction of Guard-trees under no circumstances; the way that even the first three alternatives are put in, indicating they were measures to be adopted only under exceptional circumstances.

In this comparatively short investigation, we have come upon the three contemporary kings, the young Pāṇḍyan, victor at Talaiyālangānam; the Chera of the elephant-look, and the Chola who celebrated Rājasūya as contemporary sovereigns. A number of chiefs are brought in, but they are of a minor character. The greater chiefs, who went by the common designation, 'the seven last patrons,' are referred to only as having lived and gone, and the chiefs that figured in the battle of Ālangānam itself are chiefs of the following generation, as mention of Eḻini, son of Adigaman unmistakeably shows. Round these rulers are gathered some of the poets of the first rank, among them prominent mention must be made of Māngudi Marudan, Narkīrar, Madurai Marudan Iḷanāgan, Kallāḍan and a number of others. Of these, the latter three, namely, Narkīrar Iḷanāgan and Kallāḍan come together in a particular connection. Kallāḍan is believed to have written a commentary on the Tolkāppiyam. The other two, Iḷanāgan and Narkīrar are both of them said to have commented on the work Iraiyanār Ahaporuḷ., the third section of classical Tamil grammar. The story is briefly this: that in the days of the third Śangam, the

Pāṇḍya country was afflicted by a twelve-years famine. The Pāṇḍyan finding it impossible to maintain his court asked the men of learning, who were dependent upon him, to leave the country and go elsewhere, as his resources were exhausted; when the famine ceased he got back together such of them as were still available, but found on examination that none of those that returned to his court knew anything, or perhaps enough, of this section of Tamil grammar. When he was much exercised about this, God Śiva himself took pity upon his anxiety and made this section of grammar, which is by far the biggest and the most elaborate of the Tolkāppiyam, in sixty sutras, inscribed them on copper plates and left them underneath the seat of the idol in the temple of Madura. The priest who went to clean the Sanctum in the morning found the plates which on examination proved to contain that particular section of grammar. Such a vast subject being dealt in sixty sutras made it extraordinarily brief, and could hardly be understood without commentary. So the Pāṇḍyan asked such of the Pandits as were at court to take upon themselves to write the commentary. Some of them did attempt it, but the acceptance of that which was the best was a matter of great difficulty and could be done only by an expert chairman. They could not find a suitable one and had therefore to appeal again to god Śiva himself, who indicated the dumb son of a Brahman in Madura. The little child was five years old, born dumb, and was the son of Uppūri Kuḍi Kiḷān. His name was Rudraśarman. Of the commentaries presented to this dumb prodigy there were a number; as each one was read he kept quiet; when Marugan Iḷanāgan got to read his commentary the child wept at certain places; when again Narkīrar read his comment the child was perpetually weeping in token of complete approval. The story when the extraneous embellishments are removed amounts merely to this: that the abbreviated grammar known as Iraiyanār Ahapporul was commented upon by a number of scholars. The most approved commentary turned out to be that by Narkīrar; Iḷanāgan's came next best, very much like Parimēlaḷagar's commentary on the Kuraḷ, having been accredited the best and being perhaps the only commentary now available, excepting for the statement contained in this story regarding the others. We have no evidence of the existence of Iḷanāgan's commentary on these sutras at all. The whole question now is who is this Narkirar and who was the Pāṇḍyan. A continuous tradition connects this commentator Narkirar with the famous Narkirar of the Śangam, who in another story is said to have differed from God Śiva himself in respect of a particular detail connected with this section of grammar.[10] The old story related above, queer as it may seem at first-sight, still perhaps has a basis of fact and brings Maṛudan Iḷanāgan, or Madurai Marudan Iḷanāgan into contemporaneity with Narkirar. It would be doing no violence to history at all to take these two as referring to the two poets whose name occurs so largely in the Śangam works. The famous Pāṇḍyan in

10. The poem in Kurumtogai which was the cause of this difference is found both in the text of this classical collection and also is quoted in illustration of Sūtra 2 of the Iraiyanār Ahapporuḷ (*vide* p. 39 of Mr. C. W. Thamodaram Pillai's Edn.)

whose court they flourished must then be the Pāṇḍyan victor at Talaiyālangāṇam. The commentary that has actually come down to us is the commentary of this Narkīrar handed down by word of mouth through ten generations of pupils till, at last, Nīlakantan, the teacher at Muśiri, handed it on to others. The opinion of Pandits now-a-days is that probably a successor of this Nilakanṭan, the great commentator known as Iḷampūraṇar put it in its present form. It may be Nila-kanṭan himself that did this. The modern commentary, such as it is, exhibits two layers, one which is old with most of the illustrations in archaic Tamil from the classics, with the second layer superimposed where the illustrations to the extent of 315 stanzas of poetry are made on purpose in a more modern language to be ordinarily understood by the pupils. That it is so is clearly in evidence on pages 125 and 191 of the late Mr. C. W. Thamodaram Pillai's edition of the Irayanār Ahapporuḷ where the classical illustrations are actually put into modern Tamil the poetic sentiments being the same, every detail.

The importance of these two commentaries consists in this: that the modern stanzas all of them celebrate the exploits of a particular Pāṇḍyan, several of whose achievements get to be mentioned in the course of these verses, and a close study of all these seem to indicate that they all went in praise of one and the same man. The older commentary contains illustrations, most of which seem to be taken from the classics which go by the collective name Śangam works, and this commentary criticises in certain parts the Tolkāppiyam itself, so that in the age of Narkīrar himself, the Tolkāppiyam got to be commented upon; as in fact Kallāḍanār is said to have written a commentary for which there is old authority. Narkīrar's attempt therefore was one of abridgment to make the acquisition of this vast section of Tamil grammar easy. Casting aside the legendary part of the story, we are in fairness bound to accept the existing work as the work of the poet Narkīrar, handed down through generations, perhaps in oral teaching, and committed to writing in the present form at least ten generations, may be a few generations more, after the time of Narkīrar. For these ten generations, having regard to the elaborate course of study for learning such an abstruse and intricate subject, it would be very modest to allow a period of 30 years each generation roughly. Then it would mean that the second commentary or the first edition of the commentary was made some 300 years after the Narkīrar wrote his first comment. If then we could find out from the 315 stanzas, which give a large number of historical details, as to who the Pāṇḍyan is in whose court, or under whose patronage, the commentary was put in final form, we could arrive at an approximate age. Without being much too elaborate we might say at once that this was the Pāṇḍyan who won victories over his neighbouring kings and is referred to as Nēḍumāran, who was victor at Nelvēli. He is given other titles such as Varōdaiyan, Parāṁkuśan etc. and is credited with a number of victories over his neighbours. Identification of this monarch is therefore of the utmost importance to Tamil literary history. There is the bare possibility that these modern stanzas were composed in honour of Narkiṛar's contemporary; but important considerations militate against such a view. The stanza [11] quoted hereunder gives clear indication of the existence of the Śangam, which a later Pāndyan like the Kūn Pāndya is given credit for in the Periyapurāṇam.

II :—Epigraphy

Such an identification seems possible on the facts available to us not only from these pieces of poetry that we find in the course of this grammatical work, but from other sources as well, and this has been attempted before us by the late Rai Bahadur V. Venkayya, Epigraphist to the Government of India. In the course of a study of four Pāndya grants to which we have already made reference, coupled with one or two others Mr. Venkayya, made his own reconstruction of Pāndya history, taking into

11 வேயும் புரையுமென் றேனி திறத்தின்றை
யெல்லை யுள்வின்
டோயுஞ் சிலம்ப துணிவொன்றறிந்து
தொன்னூற் புலவ
ராயுந் தமிழ்கேசரி கூடலகனகர்வா
யேயுந்திருமனை முற்றத்தியம்பு மெறிமுரசே.

Iraiyanār Thapporuḷ Com. 167.

consideration the available information from literature as well. It is on the basis of Mr. Venkayya's work that others that follow him base their own theories in respect of this matter. The grants are: the Vēḷvikkudi grant of Neḍuñjaḍaiyan, the Madras Museum plates of the Pāṇḍya king Jaṭilavarman, son of Māravarman and the two Sinnamānūr plates. The details of these plates and the way that the Epigraphist went to work at them are exhibited in his usual masterly fashion by the late Mr. Venkayya in his two reports to the Government for 1907 and 1908. It is hardly necessary for our purpose here to go through the whole of the arguments upon which the various identifications are made; and the considerations carefully offered for the identification and the difficulties in the way of their acceptance could all be studied in the reports referred to. The following genealogical table of the succession of the Pāṇḍyas based on these four and a few other dated inscriptions since published is set down here for convenience of reference in the same manner that the late Mr. Venkayya gave it.

Pāndyādhirāja Paramēvara Mudukuḍumi Palśālai-Peruvaludi.

⋮

Kaḷabhra interregnum.

⋮

1. Kaḍungon Pāndyādhirāja.

2. Adhirāja Māravarman Avaniśūḷāmaṇi.

3. Śeliyan Śēndan.

4. Māravarman Arikēsarin Asamasaman, defeated the army of Vilvēli at Nelvēli.

5. Kōchchaḍaiyan Raṇadhira; fought the battle of Marudūr; defeated the Mahāratha in the city of Maṅgaḷāpuram.

6. Arikēsarin Parāṅkuśa Māravarman Tēr-Māran; defeated the Pallava at Kulumbūr; conquered the Pallavas at Samkaramangai; Rājasimha (I) defeated Pallavamalla; renewed the walls of Kūḍal, Vanji and Koli.

7. Jaṭila Neḍunjaḍaiyan Parāntaka; defeated the Kāḍava at Pennāgadam; (donor of the Vēlvikuḍi grant), A.D. 769—70.

8. Rājasimha (II.)

9. Varaguṇa-Mahārāja; Jayantavarman (?)

10. Śrīmāra, Śrīvallabha, Ēkavīra, Parachakrakōlāhala; conquered Māya-Pāndya, Kēraḷa, Simhala, Pallava and Vallabha; Pallavabhanjana

11. Varaguṇavarman: ascended the throne in A.D. 862-863.

12. Parāntaka, Viranārāyaṇa Śadaiyan; fought at Kharagiri and destroyed Pennāgadam, married Vānavan mahādēvi, Jaṭila Nedunjaḍiyaṇ (donor of the Madras Muśeum and smaller Sinnamanur plates ?)

13. Rajasimha (III) Mandaragurava Abhimānamēru.

P. 66 Madras Epigraphist Report for 1908.

Our present concern with this genealogical table is the proposed identification of the famous Pāṇḍyan celebrated in the 315 stanzas illustrating the Iraiyanār Ahaporuḷ with No. 6 on the table: called according to these records Arikēsarin, Parānkuśa Māravarman, Tēr-Māran; he is said to have defeated the Pallava at Kuḷumbur, and conquered the Pallavas at Sankaramangai; he is called Rajasimha I, who defeated Pallavamalla; and who renewed the walls of Kūḍal, Vanji and Koḷi. That is the whole of the reference found in the inscriptions and put in abstract on the table itself. He was the immediate predecessor of the donor of the Vēḷvikuḍi grant according to this, which the epigraphist dates A. D. 769-770. The considerations on which he makes the identification are given by himself in the following words:—He takes the last four names in the Tamil part, which differs considerably from the Sanskrit portion, to be identical with the last four in the Sanskrit portion. Having done so, he states: "This is only the initial difficulty; when we get to the Chronology, the complication is much greater, because the number of dated stone inscriptions attributable to early Pāṇḍya kings is very small. Besides, I am not quite sure how and where the names furnished by the Vēḷvikuḍi grant fit into the tentative genealogy derived from the Sinnamanūr plates, which I gave in the last Annual Report." He states in another place, "it is unsafe to base any definite conclusions solely on the Vaṭṭeḷuttu portion, because a sufficiently large number of inscriptions in that alphabet have not yet been published with photo-lithographic plates for comparison. Proceeding mainly on the Grantha portion, and to a certain extent on the results derived from a comparison of the few available Vaṭṭeḷuttu inscriptions, we may not be far wrong if we assign the larger Sinnamanūr plates approximately to the first quarter of the tenth century A. D." The last name therefore of the genealogical table thus gets referred to the early part of the tenth century. This fact must be borne in mind in regard to what follows in relation to the discussion. It will be noted on the table itself that five generations intervene between the number six, Arikesari Parānkuśa of the table and Rājasimha III. Here is the whole argument of Mr. Venkayya, which it will be useful to set down here for the purposes of discussion.

"The first point which I have taken into consideration in revising the genealogy, is that the larger Sinnamanūr plates probably belong to the time of Rājasimha-Pāndya, who was defeated by the Chola king Parāntaka I sometime before A.D. 921-2. The second consideration is that the Neḍuṅjaḍaiyan of the Vēḷvikuḍi grant cannot be identical with his namesake of the Madras Museum plates, but that the former must be earlier than the latter. The third point is that the Madras Museum plates of Jaṭilavarman and the smaller Sinnamanūr plates are probably nearer in point of time to the larger Sinnamanūr plates than they are to the Vēḷvikuḍi grant. In other words, the interval of time between the Jaṭilavarman of the first two plates and the Rājasimha III must be smaller than that between the Neduṅjadaiyan of the Vēḷvikudi grant and his namesake of the Madras Museum plates. Again the Neduñjadaiyan of the Vēḷvikudi grant is apparently identical with the Māranjadaiyan of the Ānaimalai cave inscriptions. This is rendered likely by the fact of the kings in both cases being called Parāntaka. Besides, the *ajnapti* of the Vēḷvikudi grant is, in all probability, identical with the Mārangāri who excavated the Ānaimalai cave about the year A.D. 769-70. If any of the foregoing facts and surmises are overthrown by future researches, the whole genealogy will have to be reconsidered in the light of fresh facts that may be forthcoming. From the foregoing it will appear that the smaller Sinnamanūr plates and the Madras Museum plates of Jaṭilavarman cannot belong to No. 7 Jaṭila as represented in the last report. Otherwise he would be identical with the donor of the Vēḷvikuḍi grant, and paleographical considerations militate very strongly against such a supposition. Again, the numerals (up to 7), which are marked in the Vēlvikuḍi grant are very old, while those of the Jaṭilavarman plates bear a close resemblance to the corresponding symbols used in the larger Sinnamanūr plates. As both the smaller Sinnamanūr plates and those of Jaṭilavarman together mention only three generations it may even be questioned if these three kings belonged to the main line or not. But until we have definite evidence to show that these three represent a distinct family, I propose to treat them as belonging to the main line, and to insert their names in italics where they may at present be supposed to come in. It is true we have absolutely no evidence that No. 9 Varaguṇa-Mahāraja bore the surname Jayantavarman as represented on the foregoing genealogical table. But his son Śrīvallabha claims to have conquered the Pallavas, while the Māravarman of the Madras Museum plates bore the title of *Pallavabhanjana*. Again, No. 12 Parāntaka Śaḍaiyan, son of Śrīvallabha, may be identical with the Parāntaka Neḍuñjaḍaiyan, the donor of the Madras Museum plates, because the former boasts of having carried on war in Kongu, while the latter describes at length his campaign in Kongu. Consequently it is not altogether impossible that the three kings mentioned in the Madras Museum plates did actually belong to the main Pāṇḍya line, whose genealogy has been made out from the larger Sinnamanūr plates."

This long extract would show clearly the doubts and difficulties that beset the epigraphist in reconciling the various records of Epigraphy on which he mainly bases his particular investigations. But when next he comes to combine these with the evidence available in literature, it would be very reasonable to suppose that the difficulties become actually greater, and such identifications could only be made with very considerable hesitation. Even so it certainly would be more in keeping with the scientific spirit, that such an investigation would call for as a necessary pre-requisite to such an enquiry, to reconcile the various records of Epigraphy on the one side and arrive at what they have to say definitely first; then proceed on similar lines for what may be made out from literature; and then investigate the two separately to find where they would best come into connection with each other, if there is such connection at all. For such there seems certain common points. Mr. Venkayya has already pointed out that the first personage in the genealogical table is no other than the person known in literature as Palyāgaśālai Mudukuḍumi Peru-vaḻudi of whom we have a few poems in the Puranānūṟu, but from the point of view of epigraphy he is brought into no organic connection with the rest of the dynasty as indicated in the genealogical table of Mr. Venkayya. His name is drawn in incidentally to show that the village under grant was a previous gift and was known by the name Vēḷ-vikudi because it was a gift, as a result of the performance of a sacrifice (Yāga). That point must be carefully noted in this connection. The second is the Kaḷabhra Interregnum. And then begins obviously the new dynasty beginning with Kaḍungōn. We shall revert to this Kaḍungōn and his predecessors a little later. But here we might pass on immediately to number six with whom Mr. Venkayya shows an inclination to identify the Pāṇḍya who is celebrated in the modern poems of the commentary to Iraiyanār Ahaporuḷ, and let us take note of the facts stated in a previous paragraph as to his achievements and their general significance. He is given four alternative titles, all of which do occur among the 16 titles that can be made out of the part of the commentary under discussion. They are here set down for ready reference :

1. Arikēsari.
2. Neḍumāran and Vānavan Māran.
3. Pūḻiyan.
4. Uchitan.
5. Mummadiḷ Vēndan.
6. Viśāridan.
7. Vijaya Charitan.
8. Parāṅkuśan.
9. Śatrudurandharan.
10. Varōdaiyan
11. Panchavan.
12. Raṇāntakan.
13. Raṇōdaiyan.
14. Mānadan.
15. Gangai Maṇāḷan.
16. Kali Madanan.

Coming down to the battles referred to in the table, there are two such specifically referred, and one perhaps in general terms; and what is most remarkable in respect of these is that they are all referred as against the Pallavas, one of which referring to a defeat of Pallavamalla. Of these battles, the name Kuḻumbur does not occur and the other Śankaramaṅgai of the genealogical table occurs in two or three places, not as Śankaramaṅgai but only as Sankamangai, and at least in one place I fear the reading Sankaramangai will spoil the metre of the poem ; but in none of the 14 battles which can be made out from the commentary does the name Pallava once occur either explicitly or by obvious implication. The fourteen battles referred to in the commentary are :

1. Pāḻi or Thenpāḻi against the Chola (Stanza 309).
2. Kūlandai or Kaḷattūr.
3. Nāraiyūr, against the Chera (Villavan, this is sometimes used to designate Pallavas.)
4. Śankamangai (possibly Śankaramangai).
5. Vallam.
6. Ārṛukkuḍi of Vānavan.
7. Nelvēli.
8. Kōṭṭāru, where a victory was won and the Thennāḍu conquered ; a naval victory against the Chera (241).

9. Kaḍayal of Śeralar (again naval).
10. Śēvūr against the Chera.
11. Neḍungul̤am.
12. Pūlandai of Vānavar (Chera) defeat of crowned kings and the destruction of Vānavan's (Chera's) glory.
13. Villiṅam, naval battle.
14. Venmatti.

A scrutiny of this list would show that this does not contain any of the names in the table excepting the possibility of Śankaramangai. As against this possibility it must be noted that in all the 315 stanzas composed in celebration of this particular Pāṇḍyan whoever he was, there is not once any reference that would enable us to bring in the Pallavas, with the barely possible exception of 3 above. On the contrary it will be noticed in the genealogical table that number four, the grand father of this number six, is given credit for a victory at Nelvēli against the army of Vilvēli. There is very good authority for interpreting this Vilvēli as a Pallava also. Tirumangai Āl̤var in various places refers to the Pallava almost in the same terms. In the second-ten of his Periya Tirumoḷi, the ninth section is in celebration of a Pallava and a Chola who made donations to the temple of Paramēśvara Viṇṇagaram (Vulgo, Vaikunṭa Perumal Koil). In the first stanza he refers to the designation Villavan as synonymous with Pallavan.[12] In stanza 8 of the same section he refers to a victory at Nenmeli, which perhaps has a variant reading Nelvēli, and the Pallava is referred to in the term Villavan. Whether this Nenmeli of Tirumangai Āḻvār could be taken as the Nelveli is at the very best doubtful, as the reading Nelveli may not quite suit the verse. But from the other stanzas of the same section, the enemy that the Pallava fought against was the Pāndya, Tennavan, as he is referred to more than once. Thus then the Vilveli defeated by Māra Varman Arikēsari (No. 4 on the table) was probably a Pallava. That is all the point that I wish to make out at present and if this is accepted, we find that the

12 பல்லவன் வில்லவனென்றுலகில் பலராயப்பலவேந்தர்
பல்லவன் மல்லையர் கோன், [வணங்குகழல்,

dynasty indicated in the larger Sinnamanūr plates, and the others which go to support it to a very great extent, to be a dynasty of the Pāṇḍyas whose principal enemies were the Pallavas of Kanchi. For this position of South Indian politics and international relations there is not the slightest warrant in the commentary. In all the 315 stanzas there is not one reference to the Pallava, but there are on the contrary specific references to the Chera and the Chola. Four battles at least were naval battles against the Cheras, the country under contention was the Tennāḍu of the Pāndyas, that is the portion of the Pāṇḍya country which at present constitutes the southern half of the state of Travancore, which, at an earlier time, we already noticed, formed part of the Pāṇḍya country. Of these four battles, we have specific indications, but many others, almost half a dozen more probably, will have to be referred to that locality as a mere geographical investigation would, in my opinion, establish. The remaining three or four battles, such as the one at Vallam, say Pāli or Ten Pāḻi, Nedungulam, Kaḷattūr and possibly Nélvēli and Veṇmatti may be against confederate enemies, who might have been either the Chera and Chola in alliance or these and other chiefs besides. And in such a detailed statement of these, one would certainly expect to find reference to the Pallavas, if they played any part in the wars found described in the 315 stanzas. That omission which may not lead to any particular inference in the case of the inscriptions, which are merely brief statements, would undoubtedly warrant the conclusion that the Pāṇḍyan celebrity, whoever he was, did not fight against the Pallavas from the point of view of the commentary under reference; and as a further inference therefrom that the Pallavas had not risen yet to that position in which they had constantly to fight against the Pāṇḍyas at a somewhat later period.

The later famous Pallavas, whose accession to power in this part of the country became a prominent factor perhaps about the middle of the sixth century, had first of all to maintain their existence against their enemies in the north and north-west, that is against the

Chāḷukyas, and the records both of the Pallavas and of the Chāḷukyas are full of references to constant warfare and the occupation of Kanchipuram itself several times by the Chāḷukyas. The latest of which, according to the epigraphical records, was one by Vikramāditya II of which there is a memorial left at Kanchi in the shape of an inscription by that ruler in the Kailāsanātha temple at Kanchipuram during the period 733-4 to 746-7[13].

With this constant warfare on the northern frontier, it is easy to understand that the Pallavas could not have had the time to extend their power across the Chola country to come into such active hostile contact against the Pāṇḍyas. The latest time therefore to which we could possibly refer the Pāṇḍyan of the modern commentary of the Iraiyanar Ahapporuḷ is to the time of these great Pallavas. But even again supposing that this Pāṇḍya might well have ruled at a time when the energies of the Pallavas were occupied in the northern war, there is a

13 Fleet in the Bombay Gazetteer Volume I, Part 2 p. 327.

reference or two to Kongu without the slightest reference to the Pallavas and that would make this inference impossible. We are therefore driven to look for this literary celebrity to a period earlier than the age of the great Pallavas of Kanchi beginning with Mahēndra-varman as the country of the Chola and the Pāṇḍya and even the Kerala, occurs more or less in a conventional form among the conquests of his father Simhavishṇu, who may have to be referred to the end of the sixth century, at least to the later half of the sixth century A.D. Among various battles that Udayachandra, the general of the last great Pallava Nandivarman fought, figure Śankara-grāma and Nelvēli. Śankaragrāma may well be Śankaramangai, and even the Śankamangai of the Tamil poem. But there is nothing to connect Udayachandra with any Pāṇḍya as his enemy. In regard to Nelvēli, we have some detail in the grant. Udayachandra is supposed to have slain in this battle the Śabara king, Udayana and seized his mirror-banner with a peacock's tail, and he carried on the war in the northern direction against a

Nishāda chief and in favour of the eastern Chāḷukya Vishṇu.[14] It is clear therefore that Udayachandra's battle of Nelvēli could not be the Nelvēli of Arikēsari Māra Varman, the *number four* of the genealogical table. It must much rather be that of his grandson Arikēsari Parānkuśa, otherwise known as Rājasimha, who is said to have defeated a Pallava Malla among the great Pallavas. Two rulers bore this title Pallavamalla specially. The one is Nandivarman, the last great Pallava and the other is Narasimhavarman I, in the first half of the seventh century. The Pallavamalla, enemy of Rajasimha, must have been Nandivarman under this arrangement and it must be one of his predecessors that was defeated at Nelvēli by his grandfather. Therefore then for any reference to the battle of Nelvēli such as we have in the Commantery on the Irayanār Ahapporuḷ, we have to look for a time anterior to that of *number four* on the genealogical table, which would take us perhaps to the end

[14] *Ibid* p. 326.

of the seventh century under Mr. Venkayya's arrangement.

iii. Later Literature.

Leaving epigraphy aside for a while, we have some other literary aid to make an effective search in respect of this battle of Nelvēli. There is one Pāṇḍyan known to literature specifically, and whose date can with some amount of certainty be fixed, who was victor at Nelvēli. This is no other than the Pāṇḍyan contemporary of Tirugnana Sambandar, who, having been a Jain, was converted to the faith of Śiva by Sambandar himself. He is supposed to have won a victory at Nelvēli and that fact finds mention specifically in Nambiyāṇḍār Nambi's Tiruttoṇḍa Tiruvandādi (vide stanza 60). The same fact is mentioned also by Sundara Mūrti Nāyanar, who in stanza eight of the Tiruttoṇḍa Togai refers to this personage as Niṉṟaśir Neḍumāran, victor at Nelvēli. There again we fail to have the clue as to who the enemies were that this Pāṇḍya overthrew at Nelvēli. If the enemies are specifically referred to as the Pallavas, we have to look for this Neḍumāran among those, whose names occur in the genealogical table. If the enemies are not the Pallavas, there is a likelihood that this may be the Pāṇḍya celebrity in the commentary on Iraiyanār Ahapporuḷ. Luckily for us there is some little of a detail given us in the Periya Purāṇam, which elaborates the statement contained in the two works from which references have already been given. Referring to this battle all that is stated there is that the enemies from a distance were met successfully on the field of battle at Nelvēli by this Pāṇḍya in stanza 3 of this Nāyanar's Purāṇam. But in stanza 7, there is a little more information vouchsafed to us and that perhaps makes the position somewhat more clear. There it is said that it is the first of kings of the north whose army broke and fled from the field of battle, and enabled the king to wear the garland of victory along with his family garland that of the Margossa leaf. The northerners (முனையழிந்தவட புலத்து முதன் மன்னர்படைசரிய) in the one case and the enemy from the distant country (சேப்புலத் தெவ்வரெதிர்நெல்வேலி) have to be interpreted as perhaps the Pallavas and therefore this Pāṇḍyan in all probability was a Neḍumāran, who was contemporary with Tirugṉana Sambandar on the one side, certainly may be identical with the Pāṇḍyan, Māravarman, Arikēsari number 4 of the genealogical table. If the period to which this ruler can be referred on the basis of the epigraphical records should turn out correct, the likelihood of this identification becomes very great. And on the genealogical table we are left only one Māravarman, and that is the grandfather of number 4. Whether he is the Pāṇḍyan referred to in the commentary is at the very best only a guess in the absence of any clue from the grants. All that the grant says about this personage is that he was called Adhirāja Māravarman Avaniśūḷāmani, who made the earth his exclusive possession and wedded the goddess of Prosperity. That contains in it absolutely no clue to lead to this identification, but there is the possibility that this particular Māravarman, No. 2 in Mr. Venkayya's table, might be the Māravarman of the commentator.

But before proceeding further on this line, let us look about a little about the other Pāṇḍyan Māravarman, the grandson of this one whom we identify with the Pāṇḍyan contemporary of Sambandar, and perhaps a somewhat junior contemporary of the great Pallava Narasimhavarman. We have some facts regarding him from literature, which may be of some little use in regard to this particular question. He was a great Pāṇḍya, a Jaina first who, through the influence of his minister Kulachchirai and his queen Mangaiyark-Karaśi, became a convert to Śaivism. The service that these three rendered in this particular behalf had been regarded by posterity as of such high value that the three have got to be included among the 63 Śaiva devotees. Mangaiyark-Karaśi was the daughter of a Chola ruler of the time and she is referred to as such by Sambandar himself. One reference in particular by Sambandar to her is worthy of notice here, and that reference is on page 501, stanza 9 of the Madras Dravidian Book Depot Edition of the 'Tēvaram of the Three.' The Chola, her father is there referred to as 'the crowned Chola who ruled as king, well-known all over the world'. That specific reference in those terms is an indication that the Cholas still retained some power, and had not yet lost their prestige as independent rulers as from what information is available to us we know that they had done in the days of the great Pallavas. In another place, the same author refers to a Pāṇḍyan in terms which would warrant the inference that he was probably one referred to in the commentary on the Iraiyanār Ahapporuḷ. In three or four places he refers to this ruler as Tennan or Pūḻiyan, and at the same time describes him as exercising authority superior to that of the other rulers of the sister capitals. In one place he refers to the Tennan, whose rule extended over Kōḻi and Vanji (stanza 4); in another he refers to the Pūḻiyan, who was Tennavan and ruler of Kōḻi (Uraiyur), whose glory was equal to that of the northern king. In another place, he is referred to as Tennavan, who was also Śembiyan and Villavan. All these are probably references either to a contemporary Pāṇḍyan or an earlier. Probably stanza six gives the clue that the temple was built by a Nēriyan, who was also a Śembiyan, which probably means a Pāṇḍya, who had authority over the Chola, who is said in the same verse to have built the temple, probably meaning thereby that the temple had come into existence sometimes previous to Sambandar's time. If this interpretation is correct, there perhaps was a Pāṇḍyan previous to Sambandar's contemporary who could, without violence be described as having exercised authority over the Chera and the Chola, and whose authority could be considered as equal to that of the northerner, which in the language of Sambandar could only mean the great Pallava Narasimhavarman, his contemporary. Those are the terms that we actually find in the general part of the verses in the commentary to the Iraiyanār Ahapporul, and there is probably the Pāndya sovereign, the patron it may be of the commentator of the Iraiyanār Ahapporuḷ. That takes us therefore to a time just a little anterior, it may perhaps be a generation, to Sambandar, say about the commencement of the seventh century or a little earlier, and from that time which is perhaps the latest for this, we have to allow for some ten generations for Narkīrar and the Pāṇḍyan of Talaiyālangānam. We have already pointed out that an estimate of about three centuries will not be extravagant for this, and that would take us on to somewhere about A.D. 300, as the date of the Pāṇḍyan of Talaiyāngānam at the outside. That length of time is not too much nor too extravagant for a tradition reagarding the Śangam to grow. For there are two references to the Śangam at any rate of an unmistakeable character in the work of Nambiyāṇḍar Nambi already referred to. One is in stanza 49 where it is referred to with the names of Kapilar, Paranar and Narkīrar, and then again in stanza 26 referring to Kulachchirai, he is spoken of as the Adhikāri of the Pāṇḍya who instituted a Śangam. The Śangam referred to in the second need not necessarily be the beginning and the end of it and the names associated with the Śangam in the first is unmistakeable evidence of the reputation of the Śangam having been correctly handed down to this author. There are a number of references to the Śangam in the works of Tirumangai Āḻvar, who is anterior in point of time to Nambiyāṇḍār Nambi. The larger Sinnamanūr plates, one of the records we have so far been considering somewhat elaborately, have some references to this institution in it. There is one passage in the Tamil part of these plates, which refer to three incidents of the utmost importance to Tamil literature. The first is the victory at Talaiyālangānam, the second is the translation of the Mahābhārata into Tamil, and the third is the institution of the Śangam. The epigraphists, including even the late Mr. Venkayya, were led into error in regard to these three by taking this Tamil version of the Mahābhārata to be the same as the Bhāratavenba of Perundēvanār, and equating these two with another Perūndēvanār whose name figures as the one who made the dedicatory verses to several of the collections of the Śangam works. The Perundēvanār of the Bhāratavenba has a clear reference in the work itself to his Pallava contemporary, the Nandivarman victor at Tallāru. That would clearly take him to sometime perhaps in the ninth century A.D., while the reference to the Tamil version of the Mahābhārata in the Sinnamanūr plates occurs in the part of the grant which refers to a dynasty of rulers 'who had ruled, done these famous things and passed away, and then begins the new dynasty proper for which the genealogical table is possible. The late Mr. Venkayya saw this difficulty, and concluded, that "it must therefore be supposed at least provisionally, that the Tamil translation of the Mahābhārata here referred to is earlier than Perundevanar's version". No other conclusion is possible and it must be said to the credit of Pandit scholarship that the late Mr. Pinnathūr Narayanasami Aiyar, the Editor of the Naṟṟiṇai stated in clear terms that these must be regarded as distinct from the purely literary point of view. Perundēvanār seems to be rather a common name, and there was one of that name in the eleventh century, who wrote a commentary on the grammar Vīraśōḻiyam. Therefore then there were two Perundēvanārs, besides this eleventh century one, one who wrote the

Bhāratavenba probably of the ninth century, and one who made the Tamil version of the Bhāratam and also composed the verses in invocation and a few poems, just one or two, in the so-called Śangam collection.

The institution of the Śangam is referred to along with this version of the Tamil Bhāratam and the battle at Talaiyālangānam. It is not necessary that these three should have happened together in the same reign, but they were events of history at the time the new dynasty perhaps began, in the estimation of the person who drafted the inscription. That would certainly agree with the conclusions we have arrived at from an examination of literature only. Although from what is stated in the Sinnamanūr plates the inference is not obligatory that these three should have taken place simultaneously, it is clear from the whole of our investigation that the Pāndyan of Talayālangānam was a celebrity, who was associated with the Śangam prominently. His chief poet Narkirar was at one time perhaps a very important member of that Academy.

One Perundēvanār, the author of the Bharata version in Tamil is a scholar of reputation according to this body of literature, who made the collections, and composed the invocatory verses for what goes by the collective name Śangam works. Therefore then we find that the three incidents referred to are more or less closely connected, and are referrable practically to the same age, the ultimate limit of which was perhaps the age of the Talaiyālangānat-Tup-Pāndyan. Before closing this part of the argument, there is one point further that requires to be noted and that is this: The Ahanānūru collection for which this Bhāratampadiya Perundēvanār made an invocatory verse is believed to have been collected together by a Madura Brahman Rudraśarman, son of Uppūri Kilar, and the collection was made for the Pāndyan Ugrāperuvaludi. All the others must have lived and gone before this Brahman could make this collection, and arrange it in the three well-known divisions. We find the name of this Rudraśarman, son of Uppūri Kudi Kilār, associated with the commentary of Narkirar of the

Iraiyanār Ahaporuḷ. He is described there in the same terms and with the same details, and if the two are one, as in fact we have to take them, to be, then these must have taken place in the lifetime of this one man, which must have followed close upon that of Narkīrar and his contemporaries. Thus then all lines of investigation seem to lead us round and round only to the same conclusion, and that is the best period of Śangam activity for Tamil was the second and third centuries A. D.

CHAPTER VII.

ASTRONOMICAL & OTHER CONSIDERATIONS.

WE have hitherto desisted from any reference to the twin epic—Śilappadikāram Maṇimēkālai except incidentally. The two were works respectively of Iḷango brother of the Red-Chera, and Śāttan his friend. On the face of it therefore they must be contemporary with the Red-Chera and so it is from all the available internal evidence which is marshalled in the "Augustan Age of Tamil Literature."[1] We would mention here one particular point to which attention has not hitherto been directed, and that is the occurrence of two passages from the Śilappadikāram in what ought to be regarded Narkirar's commentary on Iraiyanār Ahaporuḷ. The first reference is found on page 51 of Mr. Thamodaram Pillai's edition, where the stanza quoted forms stanza 8 of Canto 7 of the Śilappadikā-

[1] See my Ancient India Ch. XIV

ram ; the other is on page 78 where the stanza quoted without number is the stanza 31 of the same canto of the Śilappadikāram. Taken along with various other quotations from classical literature, of which I am able to identify one from Māmūlanār (Page 130 of Nar. 14), another from Kayamanār (Page 118) these would indicate the class of writings from which the original commentary takes its illustrative passages. There are besides a number of references to Tolkappiam, and quotations from the Kuṟal ; as also direct references and allusions to other older stories such as the story of Pāndyan Mā Kirti (on page 155 *Ibid*). These taken together give the impression of the classical character of the older commentary which would stamp it as the work of Narkirar himself. He has other references, besides the Tolkappiam to grammarians who held views different from his own. If it is permissible for us to assume, in the absence of the commentary, that Kallāḍan[2] wrote a comment-

[2] Old verse quoted on p.4 of Swaminathayar's Puram
ஒல்காப்பெருமைத் தொல்காப்பியத்திற்.
குறைவிடைவிட்ட விரகர்கல்லாடர்.

ary for the Tolkapiam the reference may be to this author, a contemporary grammarian with Narkīrar. I shall not press this point further till my studies of Kallādam are advanced enough for me to express an opinion as to the genuieneness or otherwise of the work. But enough has been said here to indicate that the commentary on the Iraiyanār Ahapporuḷ is, in all probability, a genuine commentary by Narkīrar, the later commentator's service being confined, more or less, to throwing in the modern illustrative passages, and perhaps no more, as is clear from some of these illustrative passages being modern renderings of passages from the classics quoted by the older commentator[3] .

It is thus clear, and absolutely beyond a doubt, that the Śilappadikāram was a work anterior to this commentary by Narkīrar, and has had such a reputation then as to be quoted in illustration of some of the Sūtras, among other passages. The evidence adduced so far against such weighty and concurrent testi-

[3] See pp. 125 & 191 of Irāiyanar Ahapporul. C.W. T's edition.

mony is at least for one part epigraphical, which we have already examined in some fullness. There is one other which we shall have to examine perhaps also with some care; that is, the so called astronomical and chronological evidence for which the details are found in some of these works. Of this the Dewan Bahadur L.D. Swamikannu Pillai, who has done the most for this particular branch of work, may be taken as representative. While appreciating to the fullest extent the value of the chronological part of his work so far as they concern epigraphical dates we regret we are not in a position to approve of the method adopted in respect of these literary dates. It is matter for satisfaction however, that, to a great extent, he keeps an open mind, and that, in respect of the dates of the Āḷvars, he has thought it fit to make a complete recantation, as these astronomical details occur amidst works whose character for veracity has been subjected to critical examination, and perhaps found wanting in regard to their chronological data. In respect of his investigation, which relate to the other works of literature, he remains yet unconvinced. It is to be hoped that he will give full and unbiassed consideration to what has to be said in this particular connection. The whole of his astronomical investigations relating to this particular part fall naturally into two divisions; one the chronological basis of Indian astronomy under which come in those various considerations as to the character of Indian astronomy, how far it has borrowed its material from other sources, etc., and this is purely a question for the Antiquarian to examine, and not one exclusively for the astronomer; and the other has relation to the calculation from astronomical details, of dates etc.; in other words the calendrical parts of his scheme. We wish to say nothing more about this latter part than to remark that in regard to the few details found in the Śilappadikaram and Maṇimēkhalai that could at all be called calendrical in their character, they are made use of in a way which is very unsatisfactory from the point of view of any investigation which pretends to be scientific.[4]

[4] See my friend Mr. K. G. Sesha Aiyar's articles in the

The few details that the author mentions in the texts are taken in combination with perhaps the somewhat clumsy calendrical efforts of the commentator, who at the lowest estimate came three centuries after the author, and what is worst of all for the case, these details from this combination are altered in almost every essential particular to fit in with the fixed date 756 A. D. [5]. It is not necessary to tire out the reader by giving these details as the curious may find it worked out in Mr. Swamikannu Pillai's papers on this particular subject. We shall content ourselves with merely pointing to the grotesque conclusions to which this kind of dating leads. He has to ascribe the emigration of the Todas to the tenth century; he is driven to regard

Christian College Magazine from Sep. 1917. pp. 6-10 of the reprint in particular given in the appendix to this chapter.

[5] While admitting that there is a somewhat close agreement, deliberately aimed at by the commentator, between the commentary and the text in respect of these details, we cannot help feeling that a set of detail that requires so many modifications cannot be held to be evidence of the decisive character that it is claimed to be in points of chronology.

perhaps the Kanarese language as the elder sister of Tamil, having had an anterior development because a couple of Kanarese sentences were found embodied in the Greek farce in the Papyrus of Oxyrhynchus [6], of the first century A. D., recently discovered. No student of comparative philology of these two languages would subscribe to this contention; but let that pass. We object certainly to the freedom taken in respect of the data of astronomy found in literature for the purpose of chronology. If that freedom should be allowed, we think it is possible to find other dates perhaps very much more suitable, (such as the A. D. 201 and A. D. 202 of Mr. K. G. S.,) [7] than the date Mr. Swamikannu Pillai has pitched upon, and the occurrence of quotations from the Silappadikāram in Iraiyanār Ahaporuḷ is simply fatal to this contention of the Dewan Bahadur.

As an illustration of his method, we shall here take up for consideration the passage containing astronomical details relating to the

[6] J. R. A. S. 1904 pp. 399—405.

[7] Vide appendix to this chapter.

death of the Chera of 'the Elephant-look', which occurs in Puram 229. We set down below, for convenience, the part of the poem containing the astronomical details.

ஆடியலழற் குட்டத்து
தாரிருளரையிரவின்
முடப்பனையத்து வேர்முதலாக்
கடைக்குளத்துக்கயங்காயப்
பங்குனியுயரழுவத்துத்
தலைநாண்மீனிலைதிரிய
நிலைநாண்மீனதனெதிரோர்தரத்
தொன்னாண் மீன்றுறைபடியப்
பாசிச்செல்லாதூசிமுன்னாது
அளக்கர்த்திணைவிளக்காகக்
கனையெரிபரப்பக்காலெதிர்புபொங்கி
யொருமீன்வீழ்ந்தன்றால் விசும்பினானே.

A glance down to passage will show that it is intended to convey the intimation that, on a particular night, a meteor fell from the sky. The poet proceeds to describe the disposition of the stars and constellations as he saw them spread out in the sky at the time of this portent. The details given are, in literal translation: the nakshatra (asterism) of the day was (Krittikā belonging to Āḍu (Aries), *i.e.*, the first quarter of it; it was midnight which was dark; the constellations visible were those occupying the positions between the root of Anurādha (முடப்பனை) to the margin-star of Punarvasu (கடைக்குளம்); in the starry expanse with rising Panguni (Uttara Phalguni) the constellation of primacy (தலைநாண்மீன்) changed its position (descended from the zenith); the constellation of the day (நிலைநாள்மீன்) was just rising over against it; the old constellation (தொன்னாண்மீன்) that which had done its course was dipping into the sea; in such a situation a meteor fell, beaten into flame by the wind and lighting up the sea-girt earth without going east without striking north-(both auspicious directions).

Mr. Swamikannu Pillai tries to eke very much more out of the text astronomically than seems to be warranted, but before we proceed to show that we must refer to two mistakes of the late Mr. Kanakasabai Pillai to which attention is drawn. The first is the assumption of the latter that *the sun was in Aries* (Āḍu). The second is according to the former, the confusion of the latter in supposing the *solar Panguni to be lunar Panguni* which Mr. Swamikannu Pillai states categorically "so far as I know is never the case" that Panguni means lunar Panguni. Whether the Tamils knew the lunar arrangement will appear later. Our concern at present is another criticism of the Dewan Bahadur in which the author of the poem and his commentator are both implicated, and they are both held responsible for what probably neither had it in mind to do. This my friend brings about by an interpretation of the expression Panguni Uyar Aḻuvaṁ (பங்குனி+உயர்+அழுவம்). His own interpretation of the expression made up of the last two words of this is the 'Zenith Arc.' He complains that neither in the Śangam dictionary nor elsewhere does he find any meaning which would justify the commentator's interpretation "the first fortnight of Panguni". One would like to ask the Dewan Bahadur wherefrom he got his meaning 'Zenith Arc' for the same expression, and whether he does not actually read his own chronological-astrology into the expression. The equivalent 'Zenith Arc' has, at any rate, too much of that look, though it may not be a very bad modern derivative significance of the expression. I set down here,[8] for reference, the synonyms for 'Aḻuvan' as we find it in the new Tamil lexicon under compilation, through the courtesy of my friend the Rev. J. S. Chandler. There are 12 such given, and not one of the twelve meanings given for the word Aḻuvam in the lexicon is anywhere near 'Zenith Arc'. The actual primary meaning of the word seems to be

8 அழுவம், aluvam, *n*, ஆழ்தல்.

1 Depth ; ஆழம். கடன்மண்டழுவத்து (மலைபடு. 528).

2 Wide sea ; கடல். (பிங்.)

3 Pit ; குழி. ஆரிடரழுவத்து (மலை படு. 368.)

4 Extension, *as of a forest*, extended surface, extended level, plain ; பரப்பு.
தெண்கடலழுவத்து. (கலி. 121.)

5 Country, district ; நாடு. (சூடா.)

6 Field of battle ; போர்க்களம். வாளமரழுவத்தவுணர் கொன் (கூர்மபு. அந்தகா. 51.)

7 Battle ; போர். வாளழுவந்தாங்கி (பு வெ. 8. 23).

8 Crowdedness, closeness ; நெருக்கம்.
ஐவகைநெருப்பினழுவத்துநின்று (பதிநொ. திரு விடை. 19).

9 Abundance, copiousness ; மிகுதி. மறப்படைய ழுவமாரி (சீவக (802)

10 Trembling ; நடுக்கம். (அக நி.)

11 Fortress ; துர்க்கம். (திவா).

12 War drum ; முரசம். (அக. நி).

merely 'expanse' and no more; all other meanings of the term are derivable from this. I set down below for comparison the following ten examples from classical literature which alone are comparable with the quotation from Purananūṛu [9]. In none of these is there the slightest suggestion of anything approaching to 'Zenith Arc.' It would be impossible there-

9 1 வில்வாளழுவம்பிளந்திட்டு நோக்கி.

Chintamani 2319.

2 ஆர்த்துக் களங்கண்டோ ராமரழுவத்து.

Silap. v. 83.

3 வேந்தரார்ப்பவெஞ்சமத்து வேலழுவம்.

Pur. Vemba p. 116.

4 கூடாருடல் வேலழுவத்து ஒளிதிகழும்பைம்பூண்

Ibid p. 70.

5 அலங்கல மரழுவத்தார்.

Ibid p. 107.

6 வரைமார்பில் வேன்மூழ்கவாளழுவந் தாங்கி.

Ibid p. 79.

7 குடமலைப் பிறந்த தண்பெருங்காவிரி
கடல் மண்டழுவத்துக் கயவாய்கடுப்ப

மலைபடு. ll. 528.

8 குன்றிடம் பட்டவாரிடரழுவத்து

Ibid l. 368.

9 இரவில் மாட்டியவிலங்கு சுடர்ஞெகிழி
யுரவுநீ ரழுவத் தோடுகலங்கரையும். பெரும்பாண் 350.

10 பெருநீரழுவத் தெந்தைதந்த.
கொழுமீன். பொருந்தில் இளங்கீரன்.

Aham. 20.

fore to imagine that 'Zenith Arc' is at all an easy derivative from the etymological meaning of the word 'Aḷuvam.'

Let us then take the expression in its literal meaning interpreting the first word as standing for the asterism Uttara Phalguni, the second word equivalent to rising, the third word in its literal significance of a large collection or expanse. The significance of the expression then would be in the starry expanse with the rising Uttara Phalguni. Without importing unnecessary astronomical knowledge into the question, the expression would mean the star—bespangled sky at a period when the Uttara Phalguni was a rising star. Mr. Swamikannu Pillai wishes to know where the commentator got the first fifteen days of the month of Panguni from. Speaking for the moment from the high pedestal of our modern knowledge, the month Panguni is the month when the full moon is in conjunction with Panguni or Uttara Phalguni, that is, on the full moon day of that month whatever that be, the full moon rises in the asterism Uttara Phalguni and keeps company with it to its setting, that is, all the night. In the first quadrant of its course till it reaches its zenith both the Uttara Phalguni and the moon would be described by a star-gazer (not necessarily an astronomer or even astrologer) as rising. During the fortnight following the full-moon the Uttara Phalguni would be a little above the horizon at sunset, and has a course of rising, shorter or longer according to the day, in its journey up to the zenith. In the other fortnight of the month however, the Uttara Phalguni will rise above the horizon a little after sunset and will travel the whole quadrant from the horizon to the zenith from the point of view purely of the star-gazer. Hence it would be correct literally if the author described Uttara Phalguni in the bright fortnight as a rising star in the sense that this asterism has a course of rising through the whole of the quadrant from the horizon to the zenith. The author obviously meant this and the commentator is correct in his interpretation though not accurate from the point of view of mathematical astronomy. This may imply that the month then began on the day following the new moon and perhaps meant a complete lunation. The name Tingal for the month in these classics (note passages quoted by Mr. Swamikannu Pillai, gives us a clear lead for this supposition, and the first half of it, or what is called a puksha, is what exactly the commentator renders by the expression, the first fifteen days of Panguni. It is thus clear that if we went by the etymology of the words and interpreted a peculiar expression in a way that an ordinary scholar, without particular astronomical predilections, would interpret it, the meaning becomes not merely simple but quite clear, and it is hardly necessary to hold anybody responsible for not having done what he never proposed to do, and calling him to account for what we ourselves choose to read in his language. What is much more, to draw far-reaching inferences from passages interpreted our own way is, to say the last of it, absolutely unwarranted. We shall now proceed to a consideration of these inferences.

The more general part of his investigation as to the very basis of his own theory, is that of the late Dr. Fleet, and they rest upon more or less false assumptions. The main point of the poet in the poem just examined is, we repeat, that on a particular day at mid-night, he saw a meteor fall, and prayed, along with his friends, that no harm might befall the king, as this portended a calamity to the ruler, but as the Fates would have it, the ruler died on the seventh day. The poet simply takes it upon himself to describe the disposition of the stars in the sky at the time that this meteor fell. Those details are taken and examined with a view therefrom to find out what exactly the asstronomical system of the Tamils was. The conclusion at which he arrives on this investigation, after making the usual corrections, is nothing particularly definite in respect of the dating, as the poet has *not given the week day*, and as he has *not recorded the positions of Mars, Jupiter and Saturn*, at the midnight when the meteor fell. These very defects might have shown Mr. Swamikannu Pillai that the poet was certainly not an astronomer, not even a Panchangin, whose function it would be to do that. Nevertheless the modern investigator proceeds to put himself three questions which he answers his own way. The first of course is the omission to quote the day of the month ; the second, the omission to note a week day ; and the third, the omission to note the position of the other planets. We have already given the explanation for these omissions, but Mr. Swamikannu Pillai's answers differ very considerably from ours. To find an answer he goes back to the investigations of Dr. Fleet, and finds the answer in the position assumed by the latter that the week days were not known in India before some time about A.D. 400 and consequently the calendrical system dependent thereon could not have come into vogue before the 5th or 6th century at any rate. In finding an answer to his three questions, he proceeds to make the following remark. The modern astrologer in the same circumstances would have endeavoured to discover whether the remaining planets were likely to avert or accentuate the disaster." Precisely. The poet was not an astrologer, as many poets are not and many other honest men at the present time who know the details that the poet knew, and know no further. The further conclusions to which he proceeds are that there was a long period of time, in India apparently, 'when *the movements of the sun and the moon were regarded without any suspicion of their " influence" as planets* ; and that the Hindus also appear to have been singularly incurious for a long time as to the motions of the planets other than the sun and the moon—a circumstance which points more clearly than anything else to *the chronological origin of Hindu astronomy*, and also shows that *the practice of planetary astrology among the Hindus is of comparatively recent date.* The italics are ours, and we shall examine these two positions in some little detail.

We shall first of all examine the question of the knowledge of the week—day possessed by the Hindus. In regard to this, the first point to examine is, what exactly the nature of the week—day is and where we could expect to find reference to it. Dr. Fleet's position is " at some time not long before A. D. 400, the Hindus received the Greek astronomy, including the full list of the seven planets arranged in the following order according to their distances from the earth which was regarded as the centre of the universe; the Moon, Mercury, Venus, the Sun, Mars, Jupiter and Saturn. Above Saturn the Hindus place the stars following the Greeks in this respect also, but meaning in particular the nakshatras or so-called lunar mansions and the signs of the solar zodiacs." In demonstration of this, he starts with the assumption that the Hindus received from the western world not only astronomy but also astrology, and that the former, was borrowed chiefly for the purposes of the latter. He fixed the time of borrowing a little before A. D. 400 on the ground that the week as such got fixed in the present day order in the writings of Firmicus Maternus who wrote between A. D. 334 and 350 and Paulus Alexandrinus who wrote in A. D. 378. He then proceeds to explain how the lordship of the day of the week got to be ascribed to the various planets. The rule as found in Ārya-bhaṭṭa and in the classical astronomers is that the planets are taken in the order of distance from the Earth, which was regarded as the centre; and for this purpose the most distant is put down the first. They got arranged in this order:

Saturn,
Jupiter,
Mars,
The Sun,
Venus
Mercury and
Moon.

Taking Saturn as the lord of the first hour of the day and giving the lordships of the following hours in succession to the others, he would naturally be the lord of the 8th, 15th and 22nd hours of it; the lordship of the 25th hour would naturally go to the Sun and so on for the rest, so that we get the week beginning with Saturday and ending the following Friday. Then Dr. Fleet proceeds to state that this Saturday got somehow equated—he does not say how—with the Jewish Sabbath, and when it was adopted by the Christians of the west, the Sunday became the first by an edict of the Christian emperor Constantine in A, D. 321. He also notes that in the days of Dio Cassius in or soon after

A.D. 230, the calendrical use of the planetary names of the week days had become general in the Roman world. So the week began with Sunday, 'the lord's day of the Christians and ended with Saturday the Jewish Sabbath, which however the Jews did not use. It is thus clear according to him that the Hindus took over, not the astrological week beginning with Saturday, but the Christian week beginning with Sunday.[10] He quotes the authority of Varāhamihira (died A.D. 587) who takes up the week in this order. He proceeds to examine where it would be possible to find authority for the use of the week day and does not find it in any inscription before A.D. 484, where the day of the week Thursday is mentioned. He finds the next such instance in A.D. 664 and just a few others between that year and about A.D. 800, wherefrom it had got to be generally used. On the basis of this Dr. Fleet, and those that follow him, adopt as a

10 Why the Hindus regard the Sunday, as the first day of the week is plainly enough due to the pre-eminence of the sun, as the name Bhaṭṭāraka Vāra, he quotes from the Histōpadēśa unmistakeably indicates.

general principle that if in any undated work, the name of a week day did occur that stamped the work as a work probably published after A.D. 800 and possibly after A.D. 400 at any rate. That is the position of Dr. Fleet in regard to the week day. Let us examine the question rather closely. Kālidāsa makes a distinction between Nakshatra, Tārā, and Graha; by Nakshatra he means the constellations beginning with Aśvini; and by Tārā he means stars other than the constellations, and by Graha he is said to refer to the five planets beginning with Bhauma (Mars), both the Sun and the Moon being omitted on the consideration that they are too plainly visible and therefore constitute the first two among the planets, the other five being planets proper as the Muhūrta Darpaṇa explains[11]. The same kind of classification is followed in the Purāṇas but the Purāṇas cannot be quoted as against Dr. Fleet, who will not hear of any such, as they cannot be accurately dated. The tendency of western

11 Raghuvamś'a VI. 22 & Mallināthа's Commentary thereon.

scholars now-a-days is to date Kalidāsa on a variety of considerations, perhaps a little earlier than 400. But this is not exactly our principal contention here. There is a Tamil text which gives exactly the arrangement implied in Kalidāsa and expounded in the Muhūrta Darpaṇa. The text occurs in poem 14 of the second section of the Padiṟṟuppattu, which celebrates the father of Śenguṭṭuvan Śēra and is ascribed to an ancient poet Kumaṭṭūr Kaṇṇan[12] and the statement contained there is "you who resemble in glory the conjoint lustre of the Moon, the Sun, and the five planets beginning with Mars *which mark the days.* (நாள் கோள்.) This I believe one ought to take as a reference to the planets, and the planets of the week without the slightest room for doubt, and

12 நாள்கோடிங்கள் ஞாயிறு கனையழ
லைந்தொருங்கு புணர்ந்த
விளக்கத்தனையை.

The Commentator explains the passage thus :—நாட்கோளென்றது, விளக்கமில்லா இராகு கேது வென்னும் இரண்டும் நீக்கி நின்ற எழினும் சிறப்புப்பற்றி வேறெண்ணப் பட்ட திங்கள் ஞாயிறென்னுமிரண்டும் நீக்கி நின்ற ஐந்தையும் என்பது.

the old commentator offers the following explanation of the passage. Attempting to explain the term used here for planets, he says that the term 'KŌL' is here used in the passage for the five because the two non-shining planets should be excluded, and the two brilliant ones, the Sun and the Moon being well-known are not usually included in that term; and therefore the term applies only to the remaining five. Of course the all satisfying answer of Dr. Fleet and those that follow him would be that this poem should have been composed after A.D. 400, and therefore cannot be quoted in authority as against the general position assumed. Quite so, if the general position assumed had been proved; but there is very much more in the text than actually meets the eye. It will be noticed that the text begins with the Moon, next comes the Sun, and next follow the five in the present week day order, that is not beginning with the Sunday week. The mention of the Moon first is not forced upon the poet by the exigencies of metre. The line would read quite correctly even with the Sun before.

What is the inference therefrom ?. Dr. Fleet takes it that although intercourse, between the Greeks and the Hindus was perhaps pretty continuous since the days of Alexander, they somehow did not borrow astrological astronomy from the Greeks till all of a sudden something dawned upon them at the end of the fourth century to borrow it from the Christian astronomers of the Roman Empire. We would draw attention here to the order in which these week days do occur in a bilingual list now in the British Museum, where the seven, full planetary group is arranged as follows :—

The Moon, Sin,
The Sun, Shamash,
Jupiter, Merodach,
Venus, Ishtar,
Saturn, Ninip (Nirig)
Mercury, Nebo,
Mars, Nergal.

The reason for this primacy of the moon is due to an early notion of the Sumerians who regarded the Moon as 'the measurer', and for certain purposes as the parent of the Sun. Of these, the five planets, and the Sun and the Moon got to be connected with the chief gods of the Hammurabi Pantheon very early, and a study of the various attributes of these gods associated with the days make them somewhat different in character from what the Greeks must have had in mind when they made the equations to the gods of their Pantheon. To take only one instance, take Mercury, Nebo (Nebu) of the Babylonians. He was no doubt the messenger and announcer of the gods as the Greek Hermes. Professor Jastrow has it of him "Like Ea, [13] he is the embodiment and source of wisdom. The art of writing—and therefore of all literature is more particularly associated with him. The common form of his name designates him as the god of the Stylus[14]." This is a character for Jupiter, that agrees far closer with that of the Hindus than anything that the Greeks have to show. Although in this bilingual record the planets are not arranged in the order in which we have

13 It must be noted that Ea. is the Babylonian god that comes nearest in conception to the Indian Vishnu the deity presiding over Jupiter.

14 Aspects of Religious Beliefs and Practice in Babylonia and Assyria. Page 95.

them at present, the heading of the list by the moon is a matter of importance particularly in respect of its Sumerian associations. Could it not be that the Tamils got this peculiarity from Babylonians direct, if they could not have given that position to the Moon for the same reason that the Sumerians did? In this connection, the character given to Mars may also be studied usefully. Mars is described by professor Pinches as 'Lord of the great habitation', which according to him would be a parallel to that of his spouse, Eresh-ki-gal[15]. Of this kind of greatness for Mars, there is nothing corresponding among the Hindus, but when Nergal got to be associated with Erech particularly, he symbolised the destroying influence of the Sun and was accompanied by the demons of pestilence. "Mars was a planet of evil, plague and death: its animal form was the wolf." The Indian god associated with Mars is Yama or death, the nearest approach to Babylonian Nergal. Whereas in Greece, Mars was associated with Ares, the War-God, who assumed his boar-

15 The goddess of the nether world.

form and slew Adonis. The Indian, rather the Aryo-Indian Association of Agni with Mars finds support in Babylonian tradition. We would invite attention to the following extract in this connection :—

'The drift of Babylonian culture was not only directed westward towards the coast of Palestine, and from thence to Greece during the Phoenician period, but also eastward through Elam to the Iranian plateau and India. Reference has already been made to the resemblances between early Vedic and Sumerian mythologies. When the "new songs" of the Aryan invaders of India were being composed, the sky and ocean god, Varuna, who resembles Ea-Oannes and Mitra who links with Shamash, were already declining in splendour. Other cultural influences were at work. Certain of the Aryan tribes, for instance, buried their dead in Varuna's "house of clay", while a growing proportion cremated their dead and worshipped Agni, the fire god. At the close of the Vedic period there were fresh invasions into middle India, and the "late comers" introduced new beliefs, including the doctrines of the Transmigration of Souls and of the Ages of the Universe. Goddesses also rose into prominence, and the Vedic gods became minor deities, and subject to Brahma, Vishnu, and Shiva. These "late comers" had undoubtedly been influenced by Babylonian ideas before they entered India. In their Doctrine of the World's Ages or Yugas, for instance, we are forcibly reminded of the Euphratean ideas regarding space and time. Mr. Robert Brown, junr., who is an authority in this connection, shows that the system by which the "Day of Brahma" was calculated in India resembles closely an astronomical system which obtained in Babylonia, where apparently the theory of cosmic periods had origin.'

Donald A. Mackenzie: Myths of Babylonia and Assyria p. 199.

One would imagine then that the possibilities were that if the Indians borrowed these,[16] the chances of their borrowing from

16 Reference may here be made to the article in the Bhandarkar Commensuration volume by Mr. B. G. Tilak on the Veda and the Babylonian Creation-Epic.

Babylonia were far greater than from the Greeks, and that so late, as after Firmicus Maturnus and Paulus Alexandrinus. In support of this position, there are a few more points which ought to be noted here.

In the arrangement of the houses of the zodiac, it is now admitted that it was the Babylonian scientist first of all who divided the ecliptic into twelve well-known divisions, of which there is a noticeable distinction in respect of the tenth house as it is known to the Greeks and the Hindus. The Babylonians called it Tebet, which stood for Ea's 'goatfish.' The Greek equivalent therefor is merely Capricornus, which means the goat. The Hindu equivalent Makara is much nearer the goat-fish than the goat itself. The name of the planet Venus gives it among the Greeks the character of the woman-Aphrodite, and Venus was associated with Ishtar in Babylonia; but Venus is never associated with a female deity among the Indians, except for the fact that the Adhi Dēvatā is suppōsed to be Sachi, the wife of Indra. The planet itself is regarded as associated with Śukra, a man-rishi or a god-rishi. It is now accepted by the world of scholars that the Yuga and the Kalpa calculations (the exeligmos of the Greeks,) which begin to figure in the Brāhmaṇa period of Indo-Aryan history show very close associations with the Saroi of the Babylonians, and in the naming and arranging of the cosmic periods, or ages of the universe, there is an apparently remarkable difference between the Greek and the Indian notions, which latter are in closer agreement with that of the Irish[17]. The Indian ages are in the Indian order

17 शङ्खक्षीरवपुः पुरा कृतयुगे नाम्ना तु नारायण-
त्रेतायां त्रिपदार्पितत्रिभुवनो विष्णुः सुवर्णप्रभः ।
दूर्वाश्यामनिभः स रावणवधे रामो युगे द्वापरे
नित्यं योऽञ्जनसन्निभः कलियुगे वः पातु दामोदरः ॥

This passage from the Bālacharitam of Bhāsa, a dramatist of high reputation anterior to Kālidāsa states that in the Kṛtayuga Vishnu was Narāyaṇa of Couch-white colour. In thē Trētāyuga he was Vishnu, who measured the Universe in three strides, of a golden colour. In the Dvāpara he was Rama, who killed Ravana, of the colour of Dūrva-grass (dark green). In Kali he becomes Dāmōdara of the enduring dark of collyrium This is quite representative of the orthodox scholarly view.

Silvern (White), Golden (Yellow), the Bronze (Red, seems to be rather dark green than red) and Iron or black, whereas the Greeks would begin with the Golden and put Silvern second.

In regard to the zodiacal arrangement of the Babylonians, Mr. Brown the author of the Primitive Constellations quotes Diadorus, who gave a resume of Babylonian astronomical astrology in the following terms: "The *five planets were called 'interpreters'*; and in subjection to this were marshalled thirty stars which were styled divinities of the council. The chiefs of the divinities are twelve in number, to each of whom they assign a month and one of the twelve signs of the zodiac." This takes us to the question of the basis of the astronomical system of the Hindus. We have already pointed out that Mr. Swamikannu Pillai regards the basis as essentially chronological; whereas, the basis of the Babylonian system is astrological and perhaps even seasonal. That this is so is in evidence as "the three constellations associated with each month had each a symbolic significance:

they reflected the characters of their months[18]. This quotation is clear evidence that it was seasonal as well as astrological. We have early evidence of the seasonal character of the arrangement of the divisions of the year in the Tolkāppiam itself, where in Sutra 6, the six-fold division of the year is clearly made on the basis of the 12 signs of the zodiac, and beginning with the rainy season. The commentator, who of course is a later man explains it in the following terms: 'The year begins with the zodiacal house Leo, which is the house of the Sun, who marks time. From that, the passage of the Sun to the house of Cancer, which is the house of the Moon, constitutes the whole year. The six divisions of this year make each two months a division, and are named respectively; the rainy season, August-September; windy-season, October-November; the season of early dew, December-January; the season of later dew, February-March; the season of the mild Sun, April-May; and the season of warm

18 Myths of Babylonia and Assyria By D.A. Mackenzie p. 309.

sun, June-July. So that there is one division now which is altogether on the basis of the seasons of the year, and that it is the time-honoured division of the Tamils is inferable from its constituting the basis of Tamil division for all purposes of grammar and poetics, whether they rest upon the authority of the Tolkāppiam or no. But that this was not the sole basis could be proved by the fact that as in the case of the Babylonians, the basal idea of the Indian astrological system is the recognition of the astral bodies as the souls of the departed good, who from their distant positions exercised an influence over the world and mankind. That that was a very popular idea even from the Vedic times could be proved by the following. The Āppastamba Dharmasūtra, [19] which is an early Sūtra and without question earlier than A. D. 400, has a statement, in the chapter dealing with the spiritual advantages of having a son, that those of "Good Works" in life shine like the Great Bear (Saptarshimanḍala), high above all

[19] II IX 24, 13. Tatra yē. punyakrtah, tēshām prakṛtayah parā jvalantyah upalabhyantē.

else; as authority for this is quoted the Taittiriya Samhita.[20] The same idea occurs in the Rāmāyaṇa in a more general and popular connection when Indrajit, son of Rāvaṇa, by his extraordinary power of magic throws the head of Rāma before Sita in her garden hermitage. She bemoans the loss of her husband. She is made to state in this connection that he had joined in heaven the company of his father and there, having become a Nakshatra, he is said to see 'the whole of the Ikshvāku family of royal rishies, but, as she said, he neglected to see her in that forelorn condition down below.'[21] This is a clear

20 Sukrtām vā ētāni.

jyōtīmshi yannakshatrāṇi.

Tai Sam V. iv. 9.

21 Pitrā Daśarathena tvam svaśurēṇa mamānagha.
sarvaiścha pitribhih sārdham nūnam svargē samāgatah

divi nakshatrabhūtastvam mahatkarmakrtām priyam.

puṇyam rājarshi vamśam tvam ātmanah samavēkshasē.

kim māmna prēkshasē rājan &c.

VI. 32. 18 and 19.

indication of the general belief of men of good deeds being transformed into stars, an idea quite similar to that which constitutes one of the main items of Babylonian astronomical belief, with of course characteristic minor differences. The same authority quoted already has it that "the basal idea in Babylonian astrology appears to be the recognition of the astral bodies as spirits or fates, who exercised an influence over the gods, the world, and mankind. These were worshipped in groups when they were yet nameless." It must be noted here that these groups were general groups of seven in Babylonia. That this was so when the early Greeks came in contact with it is in evidence in the following quotation from Plutarch "respecting the planets, which they call the *birth-ruling divinities*, the Chaldeans lay down that two (Venus and Jupiter) are propitious, and two (Mars and Saturn) malign, and three (Sun, Moon and Mercury) of a middle nature Mr. Brown's commentary is "an astrologer would say, these three are propitious with the good, and may be malign with the bad.[22] That this was the early notion of the Greeks also is seen in a passage in the drama, Pax of Aristaphanes. In that comedy one character Trygaeus is shown as having just then made an expedition to heaven; a slave meets him and asks him is not the story true then, "that we become stars when we die!' 'Certainly' was the answer. And Trygaeus is made to follow the answer by pointing to the star into which Ion of Chios has just been metamorphosed. Mr. Lang's commentary on this is "Aristaphanes is making fun of some popular Greek superstition." (Custom and Myth pp. 133 Et. Seq.)

The counterpart of this notion but exhibited in more serious form is the well-known story of Dhruva, which occurs in all the Purānas,[23]

22 Primitive constellations Vo. I p. 343.

23 त्रैलोक्यादधिकस्थाने सर्वताराग्रहाश्रयः ।
चरिष्यति न सन्देहो मत्प्रसादात् भवान् ध्रुव ॥
सूर्यात् सोमात् तथाभौमात् सोमपुत्रात् बृहस्पतेः ।
सितार्कतनयादीनां सर्वर्क्षाणां तथा ध्रुव ॥
सप्तर्षीणां अशेषाणां ये च वैमानिकस्सुराः ।
सर्वेशां उपरिस्थानां तावद्दत्तं मयाध्रुव ॥

Vishnu Purāṇa I. xii 89—91.

where the boy as the result of a severe penance was found a place above all the stars and constellations. The star Dhruva is according to Hindu astronomical ideas the pole star, which, as such, is above all the other stars and constellations and the Great Bear (Saptarshayah). When this idea got mixed up with the seasonal year of the Tamils in very early times, we get the state of things,. which indicates a combination of ideas from two or three different astronomical systems; that is where exactly we find ourselves in the Tamil county.[24] There is one school of opinion which would ascribe all the scientific elements in astronomy to the Greeks, and that is what exactly is at the bottom of the notion that practically everything in astronomy, the very basal ideas of astronomy, in India was borrowed from the Greeks. To this school belongs only one Assyrialogist of great reputation and that is Professor Jastrow; practically all the rest of the Assyrialogists do not seem to support his view in respect of the indebtedness of

[24] See the concluding lines of the poem 229 of Puram with which we began this investigation.

the world to the Greeks for scientific astronomy, and more recent research seems to support the majority. Professor Goodspeed says that during the Sumerian period "the forms and relations of geometry were employed for purposes of augury. The heavens were mapped out, and the courses of the heavenly bodies traced to determine the bearing of their movements upon human destinies."[25] What is worse for this claim in behalf of Greece is the recent discovery of a document from the archives of Nineveh, which gives unmistakeable evidence of the existence of an observatory with a body of official astronomers, whose business it was to predict eclipses and issue circulars for the various ceremonies and observances that have to be made on the occasion of these eclipses. Professor Harper's translation of one of these documents puts the case very well and the following extracts are taken from it with the comments of Mr. D. A. Mackenzie. "As for the eclipse of the Moon, about which the king, My Lord, has written to me, a watch was kept for it in the cities of

25 A history of the Babylonians & Assyrians p. 93.

Akkad, Borsippa and Nippur. We observe it ourselves in the city of Akkad. ....and whereas the king, My Lord, ordered me to observe also the eclipse of the Sun, I watched to see whether it took place or not and what passed before my eyes, I now report to the king, My Lord. It was an eclipse of the Moon that took place............it was total, over Syria and the shadow fell on the land of the Amorites, the land of the Hittites and in part on the land of the Chaldees." Professor Sayce comments: "We gather from this letter that there were no less than three observatories in northern Babylonia: one at Akkad, near Sippara; one at Nippur, now Niffer; and one at Borsippa, within the site of Babylon. As Borsippa possessed a university, it was natural that one of the three observatories should be established there."[26] It is not necessary to go very much farther in regard to these. We may state, however, that according to the calculations of Mr. Brown, the signs of the zodiac were fixed in the year 2084 B. C. (Primitive Constellations Vol. II pp. 147 et.

26 Myths of Babylonia and Assyria pp. 321—22.

seq.) If then the zodiacal houses were fixed so early and if such a similarity could be noticed between the systems of early astronomical notions both of the Hindus of Northern India and of the South on the one side, and the Babylonians on the other, and if some of the minute but characteristic differences noticed between Greece and India be the facts that they are, the inference seems irresistible that if there had been borrowing by the Hindus the chances are that the borrowing was from Babylonia rather than from Greece, whatever might have taken place in later times and in scientific astronomy. Even in respect of this what we find very difficult to understand is why an astronomer of the reputation of Varāhamihira, who examines all the systems of astronomy then known to him dispassionately, and agrees with some views of one school and other views of another, should actually be charged with having borrowed wholesale from the Greeks without an acknowledgment in the face of the fact that he often quotes with approval Yavanācharya as against Satyācharya and others, so far at any rate as astrology is concerned. But that is not to our present purpose. What we wish to point out is that in the particular poem that Mr. Swamikannu Pillai has taken for investigating the system of astronomy that had vogue among the Tamils, he remarks that the month Panguni referred to is the solar Panguni and not the lunar. We wish that he were on firmer ground in making that statement. That the character of Tamilian astronomy might be regarded as solar finds support in another passage of the same Tamil classic we quoted from before, namely, Padiṟṟuppattu. In poem 59 there is reference to the month of Māśi which is described as a cold month.[27] It must however also be noted here that the term for the month used there is Tingal (moon) which suggests a lunation being the basis of the month, so that even so early the two systems seem to have

27 மாசி நின்றமா கூர் திங்கட்
பனிச்சுரம் படரும் பாண்மகள்

The commentary explains Māśi, as the character of Māśi and the expression Mā-kūr which gives the name to the poem means the doubling of the body owing to cold. Cf. Sans: Makarē Kumḍalākṛtih. (In the month of Makara people double up their bodies owing to the cold.)

been in use together.[28] It has perhaps now become clear that any general statement that the week day was not known would be very hazardous to make, and much less would it be true to apply that as a test of chronology in respect of works of literature making references to week days. It may also have become clear by now that the basal notion of Hindu astronomy was not exactly chronology although chronology did become a vital part of it later. The earlier notions certainly were based both upon the seasons and upon the astrological—animistic ideas of the stars in both these respects, showing considerable similarity to the early notions of the Babylonians and of the Sumerians before them. We shall not enter into the question of who the Sumerians were, and whether they were at all connected with the South Indian Tamils; but we might state in closing that there is very little doubt that

28. Attention may here be drawn to the passage of Megasthenes extracted on p. 67 above stating that the Pāṇḍya country was divided into 365 villages so that the revenue of one may be brought in every day. This presumes a year of 365 days.

there was communication by way of the sea between Babylonia and India at least in the 6th and 5th centuries B.C., and that communication would certainly bear the inference that some of these ideas also travelled therefrom, although we are in no position to state definitely that the borrowing was all on the Indian side. The general assumptions having been proved to be false, the whole system built thereon, we fear, cannot stand.

We would point out in conclusion that the week day as such has no astronomical significance except that in the arrangement of the week and in the notion of the presiding deity of the day, astronomers do bring in the principle of the relative distance of the planets into consideration. But this, it strikes us, is only an astronomical after-thought to explain perhaps the phenomenon that had already been somewhat in popular usage. All else connected with the week and the week day is of an astrological character associated with augury and of the animistic notions underlying that. To say more than that, it seems to us, would be saying too much.

APPENDIX TO CHAPTER VII.

We present our readers in the form of an appendix to this chapter two extracts from Mr. K.G. Sesha Aiyar's article in the Christian College Magazine, already referred to, by permission of the author, relating to the astronomical data of the Śilappadikāram-Maṇimēkalai. We have already given a short excursus, in regard to poem 229 of Puram, of our own in the body of the paper.

(1) " The passages in Śilappadikāram that are discussed by Mr. Swamikannu Pillai are found in நாடுகாண்காதை, text and commentary, and கட்டுரைகாதை. The opening lines of நாடுகாண்காதை. tell us when the departure of Kovalan and Kannaki from Kaveripūmpaṭṭinam took place. These lines are as follows:—

வான்கண் விழியா வைகறை யாமத்து
மீன்றிகழ் விசும்பின் வெண்மதி நீங்கக்
காரிரு ணின்ற கடைநாட் கங்குல்.

Aḍiyārkunallār's commentary on these lines contains the following note : 'அந்தச் சித்திரைத் திங்கட் புகுதிநாள்—சோதி ; திதிமூன்றும்பக்கம்,

வாரம் ஞாயிறு. இத்திங்களிருபத் தெட்டிற் சித்திரையும் பூரணையுங் கூடிய சனிவாரத்திற் கொடியேற்றி, 'நாலேழ்நாளினும்' என்பதனன் இருபத்தெட்டுநாளும் விழா நடந்துகொடியிறங்கி வைகாசி இருபத்தெட்டினிற் பூர்வபக்கத்தின் பதின்மூன்றும் பக்கமும் சோமவாரமும்பெற்ற அனுடத்தில் நாட்கடலாடி ஊடுதலின் வைகாசி இருபத்தொன்பதிற் செவ்வாய்க் கிழமையும் கேட்டையும்பெற்ற நாசயோகத்து நிரைமதிப் பதினலாம் பக்கத்து வைகறைப் பொழுதினிடத்து நிலவுபட்ட அந்தரத்திருளிலே யென்றவாறு.

The passage in கட்டுரைகாதை which reads as follows :—

> ஆடித்திங்கட் பேரிருட் பக்கத்து
> அழல் சேர்குட்டத் தட்டமி ஞான்று
> வெள்ளிவாரத் தொள்ளெரியுண்ண
> வுரைசான்மதுரை யோடரசு கேடுறுமெனு
> முரையு முண்டே.

relates to the destruction of Madura by fire as the result of Kannaki's curse. Of these, the two passages from the text, valuable as they are, are not obviously by themselves capable of yielding any definite result; but not so, however, the commentator's note; and if the details mentioned in it be accurate, we ought to be able to establish with almost absolute certainty the date of Śilappadikāram. Mr. Swamikannu Pillai believes that the note by the commentator is capable of giving us a definite, unimpeachable date, and he exultantly says that "between A.D., 1 and A.D. 1900 there was only one year, one month and one day, satisfying all the conditions, and that was Monday, 17th May, A.D. 756.' Let us see if this statement is correct.

The passage in question gives the following details:—

(i) The month of Chitrai in that year commenced on Sunday, Thrithiya, Swathi nakshatra.

(ii) Twenty-eighth Chitrai, was Saturday, Full Moon, Chitra nakshatra. That day the flag was hoisted for the festival of India.

(iii) After 28 days, the duration of the festival, the flag was lowered.

(iv) On the 28th Vaikāśi, Monday, the thirteenth day of the bright lunar fortnight, Anusham Star, the bath in the sea took place and the lovers quarrelled.

(v) On the 29th Vaikāśi, Tuesday. Kēṭṭai-nakshatram, which was a destructive combination, the fourteenth day of waxing moon, after the moon had set, when the sky was dark Kovalan left with Kannaki.

It will be noted that these details are not given in the text, which simply says, referring to the day of Kovalan's flight with his wife, that it was after the moon had set on the last day of the bright half, and before sunrise the next morning, when the sky was dark. Supposing for a moment the details given by Aḍiyārkunallār are correct, whence did he get them? The commentator lived probably in the twelfth century; and even if Mr. Swamikannu Pillai's conclusion be accepted nearly four centuries had expired since the composition of Śillappathikāram before this note was written. Did Aḍiyārkunallār make his own calculation or did he repeat what he had heard? Mr. Swamikannu Pillai opines that there should have been 'a continuous unbroken tradition of annotation dating almost from the date of the poem,' and the commentator in the present instance had preserved what he had obtained from earlier scholiasts. Even upon that explanation, the commentator's note could not be accepted as really of value, as after all it might have been supplied by the ingenuity of an earlier annotator, and as in the process of repetition it might easily have under-gone alterations in material particulars. However, the astronomical information supplied in the note seems to be thoroughly fanciful, as one can see from Mr. Swamikannu Pillai's paper itself. Besides, the reckoning of days in the note seems to be puzzling. We are told that the flag was hoisted on 28th Chitrai, Saturday and as we are told that the 28th Vaikāśi was Monday, the month of Chitrai in that year must have had only thirty days. So the festival, which was of twenty-eight days' duration must have closed on 25th Vaikāsi, when the flag must have been taken down, and one fails to see how the bath that concludes the festival took place as stated in the note, only on the 28th Vaikāśi. There is no doubt from the narration of the story in the poem that Kovalan and Kannaki left for Madura on the night of the bath itself, before dawn of next morning, and yet we read in the note that they left on the night of Tuesday, the 29th Vaikāśi. Obviously the note as it stands, even apart from its astronomical learning, is incorrect or not easily explicable. Is the astronomical information, at any rate, free from error? Mahāmahōpādhyāya Pandit V. Swaminatha Aiyar, the revered editor of Śilappaḍikāram, says in a footnote that the information contained in the note appears to be incorrect, but Mr. Swamikannu Pillai, while extolling the learned Pandit's candour, rebukes the astrologer who enabled that footnote to be written for ignorance of astrological calculation. I nevertheless venture to say that the conditions in this curious note are impossible and that the learned Mahāmahopādhyāya's footnote is justified.

To arrive at 756 A. D. Diwan Bahadur L.D. Swamikannu Pillai has freely edited the commentator's note. As regards the commencement of Chitrai in that year, he says that it was a day of Swati in the sense that Swati began on that day at 38 Ghaṭikar after sunrise. He admits that ordinarily such a day would be called a day of Chitra nakshatra; but in explanation of the commentator's blunder, he states that the commentator appears to have obtained his nakshatra by backward calculation from "Jyēshṭa," the star under whose malignant influence, Kovalan and Kannaki left for Madura. This itself would be enough to condemn the note as untrustworthy. What is the basis for holding that it was on a Tuesday which co-existed with Jyēshṭa star, that the husband and wife left their house in Kaveripaṭṭinam? Apparently the commentator's knowledge of astrology was so poor that he could not think of any other malignant combination except the popular Tuesday with Kēṭtai star, and starting therefrom he worked the details backward as best as he could. If the star on the first day of Chitrai has according to Mr. Swamikannu Pillai, been wrongly stated in the note, so has also the Thithi; for he tells us that the third thithi is a mistake for the first thithi. Thus this part of the note, in order to make A. D. 756 acceptable, should be made to read:—The month of Chitrai in that year began on Sunday, Prathama, Chitra nakshatra. The second part of the note declares the 28th Chitrai was Saturday, full moon · Chitra nakshatra. Mr. Swamikannu Pillai points out that in 756 A. D. in the month of Chitrai, the full moon commenced at 41½ ghatikas after sunrise the same day. Obviously, therefore, Saturday, 28th Chitrai did not combine with the full moon at all. Indeed the thithi that was current at sunrise on Saturday and properly speaking the thithi of that day was Thrayōdasi, the thirteenth lunar day. However, Mr. Swamikannu Pillai gets over the difficulty created by the commentator's inconvenient statement by inviting us to hold that by "full moon" must have been meant, a day near full moon! Why the commentator, who is at such considerable pains to supply details that will fill up lacunae in the astrological references in the text, should be guilty of such loose writing one cannot easily explain; but the suggestion is enough to stamp the statements in the note with unreliability.

Relating to Kovalan's departure with Kannaki, the note says, it was on Tuesday, 29th Vaikāśi, under the malignant influence of Kēṭṭai (Jyēshṭa), after the moon of the fourteenth thithi in the bright fortnight had set, and before sunrise. The statement is very specific; and yet in order to apply it to 756 A.D., we should again hold that the language is loose. Though the language of the note would denote that Kovalan and Kannaki left in the small hours of the morning between Tuesday and Wednesday, and that the moon of the fourteenth thithi has just set, and that further Jyēshṭa co-existed with Tuesday at the moment they started. Mr. Swamikannu Pillai finds that every one of these positions has to be given up. According to him, the departure must have taken place in the small hours of the morning between Monday and Tuesday, that is before the sun rose on Tuesday; that there was no combination of Jyēshṭa and Tuesday when they started; (as a matter of fact Anusham lasted till 10 A. M. on Tuesday); that there was no Chadurdaśi at all on Tuesday, which was on the contrary a full moon day. We are told by Mr. Swamikannu Pillai that there was an eclipse at this full moon; and we may be permitted to doubt whether, if Mr. Swamikannu Pillai's date be correct, that fact could under any circumstance have been left out by the commentator who in the passage under discussion is trying to account for the subsequent disaster that befell Kovalan. A day of eclipse is astrologically condemned as highly disastrous for a journey; and it is strange that that pre-eminently bad omen is mentioned at all, when, according to Mr. Swamikannu Pillai, Aḍyārkunallār is so scrupulous as to mention the subsequent co-existense of Jyēshta star with Tuesday, the first day of the journey; though the subsequent nāśa yoga so created could not astrologically affect the destinies of Kovalan and Kannaki. It may also be noted here that on 28th Vaikāśi, Śukla Triyōdaśi and Anusham did not co-exist, as stated by the commentator.

I have tried so far to show how in spite of Mr. Swamikannu Pillai's statement that 756 A.D. satisfies all the conditions laid down in the note, there is not even one condition that without very material alteration could be made to apply to that year. Mr. Swamikannu Pillai has absolutely brushed aside the statements of the commentator as they are, and has substituted data of his own that will support his view. If instead of the eighth century, he had decided upon any other century, the same process of editing, the same process of revising and correcting might still be adopted to arrive at that pre-determined conclusion.

(II) The other circumstance that renders it impossible according to Mr. Swamikannu Pillai to look for Śilappadikāram, before the eighth century is said to be supplied by Maṇimēkalai. The passages upon which the argument is built are these :—

இருதிளவேனி லெரிகதிரிடபத்
தொருபதின்மேலு மொருமூன்று சென்றபின்
மீனத்திடைநிலை மீனத்தகவையிற்
போதித் தலைவனொடு பொருந்தித்தோன்று,
மாபுத்திரன்கை யமுதசுரபியெனு
மாபெரும்பாத்திரம் மடக்கொடி கேளா
யந்நாளிந் நாளப் பொழுதிப்பொழுது.

Mani xi. 40—46

ஈரெண்ணூற்றோடீ ரெட்டாண்டிற்
பேரறிவாளன் றோன்றும்.

Mani xii. 77—8

பெரியோன்பிறந்த பெற்றியைக், கேணீ
யிருதிள வேனி லெரிகதிரிடபத்
தொருபதின் மேலுமொருமூன்று சென்றபின்

சென்றசென்" refers to the date of the solar month and that the thithi is not mentioned in the passage, but it is full moon. It is admitted that the expession 'the middle of the nakshatras' denotes Visākha, which is the 14th in the list of 27 stars, counting from Kārthigai. Perhaps this very circumstance should indicate that Maṇimēkalai was composed before the reckoning form Aswini had been substituted. Let that, however, pass. What is the warrant for holding that the alleged Chinese dāte for the Nirvana had been accepted by the Buddhists of South India? The Tamil Buddhists of South India had no doubt their own traditional dates based on the accounts current in the Tamil country. According to such tradition (1) Buddha's birth was in Rishabha Wednesday, Viśākhanakshatra full moon; and (3) His nirvana was in Rishaba Tuesday, Vaiśākha nakshatra, full moon. The northern Buddhists, Weber tells us, had fourteen different accounts of the life events of Buddha ranging from 2422 B.C. to 546 B.C. The southern Buddhists too had possibly a fairly large number ranging over a similarly long period. Accepting Mr. Swamikannu Pillai's suggestion that a date antecedent to 800 B.C. should be discovered for the purposes of our present problem, we find that the following dates will satisfy the conditions :—

1. Birth : 1450 B.C. Rishabha 7th, Friday, Viśākha nakshatra 30 gh. 32 p. full moon 59 gh. 18 p.

2. Sambodhi : 1415 B. C. Rishabha 10th, Wednesday, Viśākha 8-37, full moon 48-28.

3. Nirvana : 1371 B.C. Rishabha 2nd, Tuesday, Viśāka after 15 gh. 46. p. and full moon after 15 gh. 52 p. These dates besides satisfying the conditions regarding the month week day, nakshatra and thithi, also accord with the traditional notion that Buddha attained sambodhi thirty-five years after his birth, and nirvana in his eightieth year. These dates are neither improbable nor fanciful Kalhana in his Rajatharangiṇi places Kanishka 150 years after the nirvana of Buddha, and says that Kanishka and his brothers Hushka and Jushka—the Vasishka and Huvishka of the historians—came immediately before Gonanda who according to him

began his reign in 1182 B. C. I am not appealing to Kalhana's history, but I refer to him only to show the currency of a tradition about the date of Buddha's nirvana, upon which obviously he based his account of Kanishka's date. The date for the nirvana that we might gather from Kalhana's statements that have been noted above will be 1,182 plus 150 plus the period covered by the reigns of Kanishka, Vasishka and Huvishka, which Kalhana says covered one generation, (say, forty years) but which according to Dr. Luders is about sixty years. This will give us 1372 or 1392 B.C. So if we accept these dates the next question would be, from which of these three dates should we reckon 1,616 years to arrive at the rebirth of Buddha. To me it is clear that the *terminus a quo* is the date of the sambodhi, which is the real appearance of the Buddha for all Buddhists. Calculated from that date, the date of Buddha's anticipated reappearance would be 202 A. D., which will also be the date of Maṇimēkālai's acquisition of the divine bowl."

CHAPTER VIII.

CONCLUSION

As a result of this detailed investigation, it would be of some advantage to gather together in a concluding chapter the results we have so far arrived at in respect of South Indian History. That history does not take us anything like as far back as the history of the Aryans in India. The earliest historical connection is the semi-historical immigration of an Indian colony into Ceylon under the lead of Vijaya. It is this that begins the Buddhist history of the island of Ceylon itself. All that we can say about this is that, at the time this history got to be written, tradition connected Vijaya by marriage with the Pāṇḍyas. That is the only matter of interest to us. The story as it is found in the chronicle might be taken to indicate that there was a considerable intercourse between the island and the Pāṇḍyan country, and that what is said there about the whole-sale transmission of women folk from the Pāṇḍya country

Pāṇḍyan, who similarly compelled the clouds that ceased to rain to pour forth their abundance. All this which is said in the chronicle in spite of the fact that "he knew not the peerless virtues of the most precious of the three gems (Buddha, Dharma and Sangha)" is a certain indication of a community of culture between the island and the continent. It is a victory over this enlightened usurper that gave great credit, in the eye of the orthodox Buddhists, to one of Ceylon's great patrons of Buddhism Duṭṭa Gāmaṇi Abhaya. His successor got a number of great Viharas constructed, and brought about an assembly, on the occasion of the consecration of one of these, of all the great Buddhists from the various centres in India set forth in Chapter I.

The next occasion in which the history of this island is brought into connection with South India is in the period 44 to 29 B. C., when five Tamils established themselves as rulers in succession, and invasions of the island from the Tamil country perhaps became very frequent as the island itself was torn by dissensions and civil wars frequently. When we come to Gajabāhu, the Mahāvaṁśa itself has not much to say about his connection with India, but the other chronicles of Ceylon do state that he found it necessary to go to war, as on a previous occasion the Tamils invaded the island and carried away as many as twelve thousand inhabitants of Ceylon to work "in the city of the Kaveri." This story seems to have relation to the building of the magnificent city of Kaveripaṭṭanam or Puhār by the Chola king Karikāḷa. While there may be much that is historical in this body of Ceylon tradition, we cannot say we are on sure historical ground; but from Karikāḷa backwards, we have the names of some of the Chola rulers and references to some of their wars in classical Tamil literature itself. The first ruler that we have to notice from this source is Peruvirark-Kiḷḷi, who fought against the Chera Kuḍakkō Neḍum Śēral, and both of them fell in battle. The next rulers of these two dynasties were Iḷanjēt-Chenni, the father of Karikāḷa and Imaiyavaramban Neḍuṁśēralādan, the father of Śenguṭṭuvan. Then we get on to

Karikāḷa in the Chola country, and somewhat later than the date of Karikāḷa's accession to the throne or even perhaps after his death Śenguṭṭuvan Śēra was the ruler in the Chera country of the west. Between this Chera and his father, there was his uncle who might not have ruled independently, but who did conquer the Kongu country and brought it under Chera rule. This rule was further extended to embrace the Kollimalais when the Malayamān chieftain of Tirukkovilūr, Kāri by name, who was a fugitive in the Chera country as a result of a war against another chief Adiyaman Anji of Tagaḍūr (Dharmapuri in Salem), volunteered to conquer his enemy-neighbour, Ōri of the Kollimalais, and made over the conquered territory to the friendly Chera who offered him asylum in his difficulties. A successor or subordinate of this Chera laid siege to Tagaḍūr and destroyed its fortification killing the Anji in battle. This give us three generations of the Cholas, Peruvirark-Kiḷḷi, his son probably, Iḷanjet-Chenni, his son certainly Karikāḷa. Karikāḷa was succeeded actually by his son or grandson known usually as Neḍumudik Kiḷḷi identical with Perunark-Kiḷḷi, who celebrated the Rājasūyam, with whom this dynasty of the Cholas seems to come to an end, at any rate so far as we can see at present. During the corresponding period, the Chera dominions were ruled respectively by Kuḍakkō Neḍuṁśē-ral, then probably his son, Imayavaramban Neḍum Śēral, followed by his son Śenguṭṭuvan with a successor who might have been his son or a cousin, the 'Chera of the Elephant Look.' With him the Chera territory suffers considerable damage at the hands of the young contemporary Pāndyan though it recovered partly from this diminution of prestige; but with him our knowledge of the history of the Cheras ceases so far as the particular sources of information under consideration go. Contemporaneous with this the Pāṇḍyan list begins with the Pāṇḍyan Neḍum Śeḷiyan, victor over the Aryan forces, whom for certain valid reasons I identified with Ugra Pāṇḍyan.[1]

[1] I fear this identification may have to be given up; but the alternative course is not yet quite clear. I shall await the results of further analysis of this evidence for a definite conclusion.

were slightly different names. That does not mean that they came then into existence; it is only a question of the less important ones becoming more important at the time, the more important ones becoming extinct as in the case of Ori and Pāri, and some of the other chiefs losing their importance. The five chieftains that figured in the great battle of Talaiyālangānam against the young Pāṇḍyan were Tiḍiyan; Eḻini, the son of Anji of Tagaḍūr; Erumaiyūrān, probably the successor of the chieftain who went by the name Erumai, as Māmūlanār knew him; Irungōvēḷ; and Porunan. This need not exactly be construed as an exhaustive list, as some of the other chieftains of the time might have remained neutral in respect of this particular battle. This gives us a clear distribution of the powers among the various political parties in the age of the Śangam and in the two or three generations of the great literary celebrities, some of whom were considered in detail in the previous chapters and others will come in for consideration when occasion offers.

We have already seen that this part of the country made a combination to resist the incursions of the northerners. We have also noted that they kept commuication with the outside world, probably by way of the sea and this communication takes us to times long anterior to the Christian Era. At the age that we have been considering they had probably extensive trade reaching at any rate as far as the East Indian Archipelago on the one side, and perhaps Egypt, Arabia and the Persian Gulf on the other. We have already drawn attention to the great service that was rendered to this over-sea commerce by the destruction, early in this age, of the pirates and their rendezvous close to the west coast of this part of the country. We also suggested that this hostility of the south against the extension of the northern power had perhaps in it something of a hostility to the religious propaganda of the Buddhist Emperor Asoka. That is not to be taken as any hostility to the peaceful following of Buddhism, as we do find Buddhist authors, and some even perhaps of Jain authors, flourishing about the time and as there is considerable evidence of a knowledge of these systems in the south. We need not repeat here what we have already said in respect of the general condition of the country, but we may note that this age gives us, as far as we know, the conditions most favourable, to the institution of the famous Tamil Academy and all the available evidence goes to support this particular inference. There is a great deal of work that may usefully be done upon this subject further. And now that the necessary preliminary investigation has been carried to the degree of fullness to carry conviction, more work will be done to extract form the material all that may usefully be taken for the building up of the history of this part of the country and of that comparatively remote period.

ERRATA.

Page.	*Line.*			
27	9	For 'Inscriptionem'	read	'Inscriptionum'
30	13	,, 'advise'	,,	'advice'
42	15	,, Prapannamritram	,,	'Prapannamritam'
59	last line	,, 'unnderstand'	,,	'understand'
62	,,	,, 'Vaimiki'	,,	'Valmiki'
70	11	,, 'hers'	,,	'here'
86	10	,, 'he'	,,	'he'
94	5	,, कोसलाम्	,,	कोसलान्
95	4	,, Nannam	,,	'Nannan'
113	F.N.	,, 'Maoridle'	,,	'Macrindle'
114	21	,, 'The'	,,	'the'
126	1	,, 'pāli'	,,	'pālai'
133	F.N. 10	,, 'Mommhen'	,,	'Mommsen'
135	17	For 'to' read 'the' and omit 'of'		
152	19	Omit 'the Appendix on 'and read' (in my Ancient India: The Augustan Age of Tamil Literature.'		
187	F.N. 13 l. 2	,, 'Kaurajaka	,,	'Kauralaka
188	F.N. 14	,, 'Kiebhorn	,,	'Kielhorn'
190	17	Omit '2'		
195	F.N. 16	For 'at'	,,	'of'
206	F.N.	For 'S'	read	'p'
218	F.N. 9 l. 3	,, 'றேடவணிறை'	,,	'ஞேடவணிறை'

Page	*Line*				
220	F.N. 13 l, 2	,,	'ஞிட்டி'	read	'பூட்டி'
221	F.N. 15 l. 2	,,	'பெவுவல்'	,,	'பௌவல்'
,,	F.N. 18 l. 1	,,	'ஞிகிரி'	,,	'பூகிரி'
222	10	,,	'L'	,,	'll'
231	14	For	'Nitravati'	,,	'Notravati'
235	4	Omit	'by Kapilar'		
236	1	For	'Cheras,'	,,	'Chera's.
243	F.N. 3 l. 4	,,	'போல்ம்பூ'	,,	'பொலம்பூ'
245	5	,,	'Vitta	,,	'Vetta'
253	last line.	,,	'every'	,,	'in every',
254	6	,,	'seem'	,,	'seems'
256	last line	,,	'Thapporul	,,	'Ahapporul'
294	17	,,	'to'	,,	'the'
298	F.N. 7	,,	'கயவாய'	,,	'கயவாய்'
301	last line	,,	'and they'	,,	whose inferences
315	F.N. 16	For	Commensuration,	read	'Commemoration'
316	3	,,	'Maturnus & Panlus'	,,	'Maternus & Paulus
317	F.N. 17 ll. 1 & 2	,,	couch-white	,,	'conch-white'
318	7	,,	Diadorus	,,	'Diodorus'
,,	11	,,	this	,,	'these'
328	F.N. 27 l. 6	,,	kumdalakrtih	,,	'kundalakrtih'
334	16	,,	Silpathikaram	,,	'Silappathikaram"
336	5 from foot	,,	Ghatikar	,,	'Ghatikas'
340	10	,,	ense	,,	'once'

INDEX.

The numbers in the index refer to the pages of the book.

R

THE MODERN PRINTING WORKS, MOUNT ROAD, MADRAS.